# AF007

## MASSIMILIANO AFIERO

# AXIS FORCES
# 7

**WW2 AXIS FORCES**

**The Axis Forces 007** - First edition August 2018 by Soldiershop.com.
Cover & Art Design by soldiershop factory.  ISBN code: 978-88-93273558

# The Axis Forces  number 7 – July 2018

## Direction and editing
Via San Giorgio, 11 – 80021 AFRAGOLA (NA) -ITALY

**Managing and Chief Editor:** Massimiliano Afiero

**Email:** maxafiero@libero.it - **Website:** www.maxafiero.it

## Contributors
*Stefano Canavassi, Carlos Caballero Jurado, Rene Chavez, Carlo Cucut, Daniel Fanni, Dmitry Frolov, Antonio Guerra, John B. Köser, Lars Larsen, Christophe Leguérandais, Giuseppe Lundari, Eduardo M. Gil Martínez, Peter Mooney, Ken Niewiarowicz, Erik Norling, Raphael Riccio, Marc Rikmenspoel, Charles Trang, Cesare Veronesi, Sergio Volpe*

## Editorial

*Hi everybody, our magazine is getting more and more interesting, but we still need your collaboration to continue to grow and above all, to continue to improve our contents. In order to do this it is necessary that you send us your positive or negative comments, about our articles. Knowing what really matters to our readers is essential to advance and better guide our historical research. In each new issue we always try to tackle different and varied subjects, to try to please everyone. We have already received some feedback and we are trying to widen the topics covered in our magazine to all the Axis nations and to all foreign volunteer units, trying to deal with unpublished topics and subjects that have not yet been adequately covered by official historiography. In this new issue, we start with an article dedicated to Norwegian Volunteer Legion, we continue with a biography of Ernst Barkmann, a soldier in the Das Reich division and the first part of the article about the Barbarigo Battalion on the Anzio front. You will find a research article by Mark Rikmenspoel relating to the Waffen SS Kriegsberichter. Then we report the employment of the Götz von Berlichingen Waffen SS division on the Carentan front, in the summer of 1944, the third part of the work on the Hungarian armored units on the Eastern front and finally the second part of photographic reportage dedicated to the SS-Hauptsturmführer Hans-Jörg Hartmann. Happy reading to everyone and see you in the next issue.*

*Massimiliano Afiero*

## Contents

in World War Two 1939-1945

# The Volunteer Legion Norwegen
## by Erik Norling

Propaganda poster for Norwegian Legion.

Norwegian Volunteers lined up waiting to provide their generality to enlist in the Legion, Summer 1941.

The *Volunteer Legion Norwegen* was established by Vidkun Quisling's political party, *Nasjonal Samling*, after receiving the necessary authorization from the German administration on 27 June 1941. On 29 June, the German representative in Norway, *Reichskommissar* Terboven, announced the formation of a Norwegian unit to fight against the Communism along with the Finns (and Germans).

The purpose of the Legion was

1) to enable the Norwegians to fight the Soviets in their own national formation;

2) to rebuild the Norwegian Army to prepare the departure of the German occupants and

3) to provide publicity for the "New European Order" and its multi-national crusade against communism.

In order to attract volunteers a major recruiting campaign was immediately launched with all of the trappings. The Legion was described as a "expeditionary force" more to assist the Finns (for whom their was greater sympathy since the Winter War 1939-1940) than the Germans. At first, little or no mention of the fact that the Legion would be administered by the *Waffen-SS*. A number of celebrities actively participated in recruiting activities for the Legion. Recruiters of the Norwegian emphasized its "non-political" status (i.e. not particular National Socialist nature) and its nationalist, patriotic role. Promises were made however that it proved impossible to keep. For instance, even though Norwegian Army uniforms had been promised, it was simply not possible to use uniforms markedly different from that of the Germans in a combat situation under

German leadership. Again it was not realistic just to utilize former members of the Royal Norwegian Army in the heavy fighting on the Eastern Front just based on their former status. Ability, not previous ranking, was what counted the most in life-or-death situations. On 12 July 1941, the first volunteers were assembled in *Bjölsen Skole*, a school close to Oslo, and a few days after they left for the Gulskogen Camp were the Legionaries received their uniforms and the companies were formed.

Norwegian volunteers still in civilian clothes at the Bjölsen school, July 1941.

Gulskogen, Summer 1941: Norwegian volunteers in march.

*Legions-Sturmbannführer* **Jörgen Bakke, first commander of the *'Viken'* Battalion, 1941.**

The idea was to develop the Legion as an infantry regiment with seven battalions (one for each administrative region of the country), amounting at least 7.000 volunteers. The first one was named *Viken*. Each battalion was to consist of 3 light (infantry) companies and 1 heavy (machine-guns/mortars) company. The command was given to a Norwegian staff officers led by the *Major* Finn Kjelstrup, who was appointed by Quisling. *Major* Jörgen Bakke was named commander of the first battalion.

## Training

The Legion volunteers left for Germany on 29 July 1941 and were sent to the Fallingbostel training camp near Hamburg for basic training. The training was directed by a German *Ausbildungsstab* (Instruction staff) of the *Waffen-SS* led by *SS-Hstuf*. Fick. Problems began to develop immediately between both *Major* Bakke and the Oslo Staff as well between the *Waffen-SS* trainers and the Norwegian officers of the Legion, but the formation of the unit continued. Due to lack of volunteers (only 1.300 had come to Germany), the *SS-Führungshauptamt* (*Waffen-SS* Main Office) decided to organize the Legion as a reinforced battalion. A German Berater (Advisor) was then assigned to each Norwegian unit commander. Following the initial disputes between the Germans and Norwegians, some of the older Norwegian officers resigned and they were then replaced in the command of the companies by younger and motivated officers.

Fallingbostel, Summer 1941: Norwegian volunteers in march with the fatigue uniforms.

Fallingbostel, Summer 1941: Norwegian volunteers train with a 37mm anti-tank piece.

The *Leg.-Stubaf.* Quist, new commander of the Norwegian Legion. On his uniform, are clearly visible the collar tab with the lion and the embroidered badge of the *Hird* on the sleeve just up the cufftitle.

In December 1941, the Oslo Staff was dissolved and the command of the Legion was handed over to *Major* Bakke, who a few days afterwards was transferred to the SS division *Wiking*, where several hundreds Norwegians were already fighting. Many of these were among the first Norwegian volunteers who had joined the division in January 1941. Quisling was now able to appoint *Major* Arthur Quist, a loyal and nationalistic officer, to command the Legion. He would remain CO during the entire life of the unit.

## Freiwilligen Legion Norwegen

The official unit title was *Freiwilligen Legion Norwegen* and, despite that they were administered by the *Waffen-SS*, the volunteers were not considered members of the *Waffen-SS* and the prefix *Legion* instead of SS was used before the rank designation (i.e. *Legion-Unterstürmführer* instead of *SS-Unterstürmführer*). Even so, the volunteers always prefered to use the Norwegian ranks and the "*Major*" was always "*Major*" despite the German rank (*Legion-Sturmbannführer*). In addition, the Norwegians did not use the SS runes on their uniform collar patches, instead they utilized the Norwegian lion emblem. They were authorized to wear a cuff title on the lower left arm with the name of their unit along with a sleeve shield bearing the national colors (during the instruction time) or the

St.Olaf's Cross emblem of the *Hird*, the paramilitar branch of *Nasjonal Samling*. The first battalion was officially inaugurated on 3 October 1941, during a colourful ceremony at the Fallingbostel Camp with Vidkun Quisling presiding over the ceremony.

**The Norwegian Legion flag, during the oath ceremony in Stettin, december 1941.**

**Transfer of Norwegian volunteers on trucks to the front operating area, February 1942.**

Colors were presented and a revised oath-of-allegiance to Adolf Hitler, as head of the military forces fighting against Communism.

## On the front of Leningrad

After seven frustrating months of waitings for the volunteers, preparations were finally made to send the Legion to the Front. The Germans had agreed to send them to the Finnish sector but this was cancelled due to transport and organizational difficulties, (the ice covered the Baltic Sea this winter). So in February 1942 the Norwegians were instead sent to the Leningrad front. The Legion, close to 1,000 men strong, arrived on 28 February at Finnskoe Korojwa, where it assumed positions under the command of the *Waffen-SS* but with a German *Wehrmacht* unit, the 409th Regiment. Later it become part of the 2nd SS Motorized Infantry Brigade, in which some of the other national legion, (Flemish, Dutch and Latvian), were serving.

A Norwegian volunteer, with a machine gun, in white camouflage clothing.

A Norwegian legionnaire with Winter clothing and *Mauser K98*, during a reconnaissance action, among the Soviet trenches.

A Norwegian patrol on the Leningrad front, 1942.

In terms of offensive action, this northern sector of the Russian Front was static as far as the German were concerned; however the Soviets engaged in continual probing attacks against the German defenses with the objective of freeing Leningrad from encirclement, so the action was hot and heavy at times. The Norwegian were immediately given scout and assault troop assignments that resulted in numerous bloody small-scale engagements. In April, the Legion now at Urizk close to the Gulf of Finland, was attacked by heavy Russian forces and lost many soldiers, including three officers. By May 1942, the Legion had lost almost 50% of its personnel in essentially minor actions, (and this in a sector that was supposedly "quiet"!). At this time the Legionaries were awarded their first combat decorations, (a sizable quantity of them!). The Legion CO, Quist, received the Iron Cross, 1st Class, and many were to follow. In the spring of 1942, Vidkun Quisling paid a visit to the Legion and in July of that same year, *Reichskommissar* Terboven and the General Secretary of *Nasjonal Samling*, Rolf Fuglesang also visited the unit positions. The Legion was relocated to a quieter area, Gongosi, where it stayed until wintertime.

The *Leg.-Unterscharführer* William Harry Andresen.

May 1942: Vidkun Quisling, during his visit to the Legion, meet the newly decorated Norwegian volunteers.

A Norwegian anti-tank gun ready to open fire. The men are in white camouflage clothing, January 1943.

In the autumn 1942, reduced to less than 600 men due to casualties, the Legion received reinforcements in the form of the 1st SS Company of the Norwegian Police led by the NS Minister Jonas Lie, who was also head of the Germanic SS in Norway. He had served in the *Leibstandarte SS Adolf Hitler* during the Balkan Campaign of 1941.

In January 1943, the batteries of the Legion's 14th Anti-tank Company were assigned to the *Spanish Blue Division*, the Dutch Legion and the Latvian Brigade, which were also serving in the 2nd SS Brigade. The Norwegian gunners, with 75mm field pieces, supported these troops in the violent battles that raged in this sector into February 1943, as the Russians tried to liberate Leningrad. The Norwegians (almost

50 all told) were almost all killed or wounded. The other units took high losses as well as the *Spanish Blue Division* losing over 2,000 men!!

A Norwegian anti-tank gun on Leningrad front, February 1943.

Soviet tanks destroyed and abandoned in front of the Norwegian defensive positions.

Norwegian Volunteers return to Norway, 1943.

All of the German High Commanders, including the *Reichsführer-SS* Heinrich Himmler himself, paid tribute to the bravery of the Norwegians.

At the beginning of March 1943, the Legion was withdrawn from the front and sent to Mitau, where the Replacement Company and field hospital were located. Around 500 Legionaries left the frontlines but they had to leave behind the bodies of 180 comrades killed in action over the previous months. Of these, 158 were buried in the cemetery of the Heros at Duderhof West (Krassnoje Selo). On May 20, 1943, the Legion, along with other Germanic Legions, was dissolved. 300 of the survivors chose to re-enlist in the newly formed SS-Regiment *Norge*. Many of the Legionaries made their way to Norway where they entered into the administration of the NS-

Quisling greets the Legion veterans in Oslo, 1943.

Party, or re-enlisted in the other *Waffen-SS* units, chiefly the SS-*Ski Battalion Norge*, which saw action with the *6.SS Mountain Div. Nord* on the Finnish Front.

Others served in the Rgt *Norge* of the *11.SS Division Nordland*, and they saw action from Croatia to Narwa, and from Kurland to Berlin and even Budapest. They took part in some of the bloodiest battles ever to be seen in European military history.

Special mention to be made of the approximately 40 legionaries that graduated from the European Military Academy at Bad Tölz, where *Waffen-SS* officers were trained. Of these, at least 30 were killed in action during the war, proving themselves to be 'real' SS men.

## Order of battle
*Freiwilligen Legion Norwegen*
**1 January 1942 – 20 May 1943**

| | | |
|---|---|---|
| Battalion HQ | *Leg.-Stubaf.* Arthur Quist |  |
| War Reporters Detachment | *Leg.-Oscha.* Bang | |
| 1 (Inf.) Co. | *Leg.-Ostuf.* Olaf Lindvig (Wounded) | |
| | *SS-Ostuf.* Radbruch (German) | |
| | *SS-Ostuf.* Ziegler (German) | |
| | *Leg.-Ustuf.* Sophus Kahrs | |
| 2 (Inf.) Co. | *Leg.-Ostuf.* Karsten Sveen (Wounded) | |
| 3 (Inf.) Co. | *Leg.-Ostuf.* John Braseth | |
| | *Leg.-Ustuf.* Einar Höve (KIA) | |
| 4 (heavy) Co. | *Leg.-Hstuf.* Ragnar Berg (KIA) | |
| | *Leg.-Ostuf.* Njaal Reppen | |
| 14.(Anti-tank) Co. | *Leg.-Hstuf.* Finn Finson | |
| | *Leg.-Ostuf.* Tor Marstrander | |
| 1 SS Police Co. | *SS-Hstuf.* Jonas Lie (from Sept. 1942) | **Jonas Lie and Himmler.** |

## Bibliography
Massimiliano Afiero, "*Den Norske Legion*", Associazione Culturale Ritterkreuz
Erik Norling, "*De los fiordos a las estepas: la legion SS Noruega en el Frende del Este (1941-1943)*", Garcia Hispan Editor
Richard Landwehr, "*Frontfighter; The Norwegian Volunteer Legion of the Waffen-SS, 1941-1943*", Merriam Press

# SS-Oberscharführer
# Ernst Barkmann
### by Peter Mooney

*SS-Sturmmann* **Barkmann.**

*SS-Rottenführer* **Barkmann.**

Barkmann was born on 25 August 1919 in Kisdorf, within the Holstein area. He was the son of a farmer and that aspect became important in various aspects of his history. He became a member of the *Hitler Jugend* at the start of May 1932, therefore eligible to wear the Old Fighter's Chevron, although no images appear to show him with that. He was listed as the inheritor of his father's farm and his father was teaching him the trade from a young age. Barkmann also attended agricultural school, as well as taking part in a young-farmer's exchange program to Denmark and Sweden in the summer of 1938. That was followed in November 1938 when he moved to the *R.A.D.*, staying there until late-March 1939. Back in mid-February 1939, he received a reply from the *Leibstandarte*, covering his question of how long he would have to serve in their ranks. They responded by saying that his request to only serve two-years (presumably in connection to the family farm?), would require a letter from his father, as the *Leibstandarte* required a four-year service obligation. They went on to say that, if the letter was not forthcoming, they would have to withdraw his voluntary application to join them. What is even more puzzling, is that he became a member of the *SS-Regiment Germania* from the start of April! He went through his basic training and was ready in time for the opening campaign in World War Two.

He went into Poland as part of the *9.Kompanie* and would stay with them until early-1942; whilst in Poland he received his first wound. In 1940 he went westwards through Holland, Belgium and France, receiving a promotion to *SS-Sturmmann* at the start of June. After the west, his Regiment became part of the newly raised *SS-Division Wiking*. His next campaign was the advance into the Soviet Union in July 1941. On the first day of that month, he was moved to the rank of *SS-Rottenführer*. On the 14th of July he was awarded the Second Class Iron Cross, then on the 23rd, he was wounded again and sent away from the frontline (Silver Wound Badge followed for that).

*SS-Unterscharführer* **Barkmann.**

*SS-Uscha.* **Barkmann on guard, 1943.**

He was sent to the Replacement Battalion for Germania and whilst there, he received the Infantry Assault Badge, awarded on the 18th of February 1942. In April, he moved to the Panzer Battalion of *SS-Division Reich,* initially serving with their *2.Kompanie.* Whilst in France, his Kameraden received their Russian Front Medal. That award is not listed for Barkmann, nor is he seen wearing it in any of the later war images of him. That could be due to the fact that his wound removed him from that theatre within the first month of fighting?

When he returned to Russia in 1943, he was part of a *Panzer III* crew, which then quickly became command of his own tank (number 221). That vehicle was knocked out during the Kharkov fighting, but Barkmann and his crew survived. After Kharkov, his Battalion was sent to Germany to train on the new Panther tank; Barkmann moved to the *4.Kompanie* in mid-1943. Fighting with them throughout the remainder of 1943 in the Ukraine, he received a promotion to *SS-Unterscharfuhrer* in September. He was part of the contingent that was sent westwards at the end of 1943.

Being part of the main *Das Reich Division,* he helped ensure he and his crew were ready for the upcoming Allied invasion; he was commanding Panther number 421 by then. Fighting against American forces during July, he conducted a significant action in the closing days of that month, which resulted in him being proposed for the award of the Knight's Cross. Barkmann had been awarded the First Class Iron Cross on the 1 st of August, which 'allowed' the Knight's Cross recommendation to follow suit. That short document came from the headquarters of the *7.Armee* on the 7th of August (Rudolf Enseling's and Fritz Langanke's proposals were on the same document) and covered: 'SS-Unterscharführer *Barkmann, 4./SS-Pz.Rgt.2, was left behind with his* Panther *on the 27th of July 1944 to guard two broken down vehicles north of Canisy. During the night of the 28th and 29th of July 1944, the vast backward moves of the Division completely cut him off from his own forces. He destroyed one tank and started his march towing the other Partly crossing American lines and partly driving amongst them at night, he knocked out 14 enemy tanks and reached his own lines on the 30th of July 1944.'*

Barkmann and his *Panther* in Normandy, 1944.

Barkmann with *Ritterkreuz*, 1944.

*SS-Oberscharführer* Barkmann.

That proposal was approved on the 27th of August 1944. On the 31st of August, he received a promotion to *SS-Oberscharführer,* backdated to the 1st of August. Barkmann continued his combat record during the Ardennes, where he inflicted further tank losses on the enemy. He was in another *Panther* tank, that one carrying the number 401. He took part in a well-documented advance through on the 24th of December, with luck and bluff playing their part in his advance. The initial advance by the *I.Battalion* met with enemy resistance and suffered some initial damage and losses. Barkmann adjusted and used a culvert alongside the main road to advance further forwards.

*SS-Oberscharführer* **Barkmann.**

*SS-Oscha.* **Barkmann and his crew, 1944.**

He moved towards some woods and came across a tank alongside him. He was under the impression that this was a friendly vehicle, but quickly determined that it was an American *Sherman*. Quick maneuvering brought his tank into a position to be able to knock this enemy vehicle out – at a distance of three feet! He was almost immediately engaged by a further 2 tanks, one of these was knocked out. Advancing further forwards in the moonlit and clear night, he came across the sight of nine enemy tanks with their guns facing his flank. He bluffed his way through and did not halt or stop. Once he was past the majority of them, he ordered a halt and and the turret was turned 90 degrees to face the now exposed enemy tank at the end of this line up. Before he could order the main gun to fire, the crews of the enemy tanks bailed out. He decided to carry on without engaging them, but in the subsequent advances by *Panthers* of the Battalion, these nine enemy Shermans were all knocked out where they stood. His advance brought him right through the middle of Manhay and into the centre of the lined up tanks of the U.S. 7th Armoured Division, the 82nd Airbourne Division and the 75th Infantry Divisions. Barkmann estimated at least 80 tanks neatly lined up one after the other. He wasted no time in maintaining the advance, right through American soldiers, who had the courtesy to move out of his path – none of them realizing that he was an enemy tank, until he had travelled past them; luck playing a part once again! A collision with an American Jeep, caused him to become temporarily entangled with one of the Shermans further down this seemingly endless column, but he managed to get himself free. Using smoke canisters, he made it out of Manhay without any hits. He was pursued, but managed to take out any of the enemy vehicles that got close. At this was going on, some of the Panthers from the Battalion had made it into Manhay and they proceeded to engage the countless targets, which resulted in this objective coming into German hands. Barkmann himself had turned around and moved back into Manhay, where he encountered infantry from his Division.

**German *Panther* during Ardenne offensive, January 1945.**    ***SS-Ostubaf.* Joachim Peiper**

*SS-Oberscharführer* **Barkmann.**

During that Ardennes battle, Barkmann was credited with another seven tanks, 3 more armoured vehicles and two Jeeps. As with most other Germans unit in that area, they disengaged from the enemy in January and begun their journey to the southwest and Hungary. For Barkmann, he was awarded the Gold Wound Badge on the 25th of January 1945. His final fighting was in Austria where he spent a short stint as part of Joachim Peiper's Panzer Regiment. That encounter turned out to be relatively 'interesting'. He was part of a unit that had ten Panthers and they were initially fighting alongside Wehrmacht armour. They managed to make it through enemy spearheads, after losing the *Wehrmacht* vehicles, who were knocked out. In doing so, they made contact with the *1.SS-Panzer Division 'LSSAH'*, in particular, the *Panzer Regiment* under *SS-Obersturmbannführer* Joachim Peiper. Peiper's reputation preceded him and he was a Knight's Cross with Oakleaves and Swords holder by that stage. He wanted to requisition the *Das Reich* Panthers, but the commander of Barkmann's small group refused. They did however, proceed to fight with Peiper's tanks against the Russians. During these late-March 1945 days, Barkmann and his *Das Reich* panzer Kameraden, proved their worth to the highly experienced Peiper. Continuing to fight in close-range tank duels, Barkmann's tank is credited with the destruction of a further nine Russian tanks, including a heavy Josef Stalin variant.

*SS-Oberscharführer* **Barkmann**.

Due to direct hits, his own tank had to be left behind, but not before he and his crew destroyed it with charges. When it came time to part ways with the panzer men from the *Leibstandarte*, they done so under very friendly terms. By the war's end, Ernst Barkmann was credited with the destruction of more than eighty enemy tanks, one hundred and thirty other armoured vehicles and forty anti-tank guns. He is also listed as holding the Tank Assault Badge '25' and '50', for having taken part in that number of armoured engagements, but the exact dates of those awards are not listed (we can presume 1944 and 1945, respectfully?). In the closing days of the conflict, he made his way home on foot from Austria to northwest Germany. According to some reports, the British controlled that sector and he was placed as a prisoner of war until 1947. However, Barkmann himself stated that he was not put in a prisoner of war camp, but allowed to work the family farm. During one of our conversations, he also mentioned that British soldiers entered his father's farm when he worked there and questioned him. That would tie in with the fact that he retained his awards and overalls? Whatever that immediate post-war situation was, he worked on the family farm and following that, became a volunteer fireman and also the Mayor of the village where he lived.

**Peter Mooney with Ernst Barkmann and his *Ritterkreuz*.**

The Author was lucky enough to meet with Herr Barkmann on a few occasions at his home, but also at a HIAG reunion. During those visits, he showed me his original Knight's Cross, as well as his superb photo collection. The highlight of those trips however, was being able to not only see his original wartime one-piece camouflage overalls, but being offered the chance to try these on by Herr Barkmann – an offer that was quickly accepted and the moment photographed for posterity! This former tank-ace of the *Waffen-SS* lived until the 27th of June 2009.

# The Barbarigo Battalion on the Anzio Front
by Massimiliano Afiero

Valerio Borghese reviews the *Barbarigo* battalion.

Admiral Sparzani greets the departing *Barbarigo*.

The *Barbarigo* parades through the streets of La Spezia.

## The first to fight

*"Barbarigo is the first unit entrusted with the responsibility of vindicating the honor of our arms, do not forget, we all have to feel this responsibility on our shoulders, everything has to spur us in the fight, none of us fears death. You must know how to die and know how to die with discipline. You of the 'Barbarigo' are entrusted with a luminous tradition. Add even more glory to glory. In the banner that today you brought to the defense of Rome are three symbols. Tenth Flotilla MAS. From the beginning of the war, the 'Tenth' with tenacious will brought destruction and death to the enemy units sheltered in the well defended ports and on September 8, refused the treason and the disgrace of the armistice by holding the flag high and continuing the fight. San Marco: a shining name which for twenty years has been a cry of recovery, of struggle and of victory, Barbarigo, a glorious name linked to two of the most beautiful victories of the Navy in the waters of the Atlantic. So let glory be added to glory. "* With this speech, the commander of the Tenth MAS, Junio Valerio Borghese, greeted the men of Barbarigo in La Spezia before their departure for the Anzio front, on February 19, 1944. The Undersecretary of the Navy, Admiral Sparzani, greeted the battalion, which paraded through the streets of La Spezia,

warmly acclaimed by the population, happy to see again Italian soldiers go to defend the country. The *'Barbarigo'* battalion, initially called *'Maestrale'*, was one of the first Navy Infantry units of the 'Decima' to be established in La Spezia, at the San Bartolomeo barracks, in November 1943. Its commander was navy Lieutenant Umberto Bardelli[1]. In January 1944, in memory of the submarine of Commander Enzo Grossi[2], it was given the name of *'Barbarigo'*.

**Corvette Captain Bardelli.**

**The *Barbarigo* war flag.**

**La Spezia, 19 February 1944: marines of *Barbarigo* before departure.**

Of its four companies, IIa and IVa had been trained in San Bartolomeo, while the Ia and IIIa had been transferred for training in Cuneo, to the San Dalmazzo barracks.

Rome, 28 February 1944: a young marine of *Barbarigo* during a ceremony.

In mid-February, the battalion was regrouped again in La Spezia. On 19 February 1944, the unit received the combat flag from Commander Borghese and on the 20th, left for the front of Anzio-Nettuno, where the Anglo-Americans had created a bridgehead after the landing occurred on 22 January 1944 (operation *Shingle*). The *Barbarigo* order of battle, in February 1944, was as follows[3]:

Commander: Corvette Captain Umberto Bardelli
Deputy Commander: Captain S.M. Giuseppe Vallauri
Headquarters company: Second Lieutenant Mario Bordogna
1st company ('*Decima*'): Captain Giulio Gay
2nd company ('*Sciré*'): Lieutenant Domenico Trettene
3rd company ('*Iride*'): Lieutenant Mario Honorati
4th company ('*Tarigo*'): Captain Bruno Malferrari

## In the eternal city

Aboard their vehicles, passing through Florence, Siena, Orvieto, Viterbo, the marines arrived in Rome, after having suffered under Allied air bombardments. During a stop in Siena, more than two hundred students from the local officer school of the GNR, joined the marines, eager to fight immediately in the front line. In the Italian capital, the marines stayed a few days, staying at the '*Graziosi Lante*' barracks in Piazza Randaccio, where *Maridist*, the Roman detachment of the Republican Navy, was located.

The German military commander of Rome, General Kurt Maeltzler, reviews the men of *Barbarigo*, February 1944.

To try to keep up the morale of men, but also for reasons of propaganda, some parades were organized, attended by high Italian and German military officers. On 21 February, during an official ceremony, the men of Barbarigo were given, by the officers and the commander of the PAI (Italian Africa Police), vaguely African-style daggers, which proved to be very useful in subsequent fighting on the bridgehead of Anzio. Commander Bardelli took advantage of those days of waiting to improve the armament and equipment of his units: the battalion was equipped with good individual armament, based on the Beretta submachine gun, but lacked heavy weapons, machine guns and mortars. It was then that a captain of the Grenadiers of Sardinia, Alberto Marchesi, intervened. After September 8, 1943, he had been busy recovering all the material left behind by the fleeing Italian units, in the warehouses of the Ferdinando di Savoia barracks in Pietralata. From there, the captain Bardelli was able take everything he wanted and also brought with him Captain Marchesi, entrusting him with the role of officer in charge of supplies.

## On the bridgehead

**German infantrymen on the Anzio front, passing by a destroyed 'Ferdinand', March 1944.**

On the evening of March 3, 1944, the marines finally left for the front. On board trucks, after passing Velletri, they stopped at Sermoneta, where there was a German observation post which dominated all the Allied landing beachheads. The marines could thus observe the distant exchanges of the opposing artillery. Bardelli immediately ordered the deployment of the service units to a house near the road junction for Littoria; the field kitchens were set up and in the same area the supply base was also established, referred to by the Germans as the 'tross

in World War Two 1939-1945

Valentini', from name of the officer who directed it. In Doganella, the field hospital was installed under the guidance of Lieutenant Maggiani. Soon after, Commander Bardelli, accompanied by the deputy commander, Captain Vallauri and the adjutant major, Lieutenant Urbano Rattazzi, went to confer with the *Oberst* Friedrich von Schellerer, commander of a combat group of 715. Infantry-Division. This division, under the orders of *Generalleutnant* Hans-Georg Hildebrandt, defended the entire southern sector of the bridgehead, from Cisterna to the sea. Originally created as a static infantry division with garrison duties, it was sent in a hurry to Nettuno after the Allied landing, not properly equipped: most of its weapons were war booty and its artillery regiment included only one group of 105 mm howitzers and a group of 7.62 cm guns.

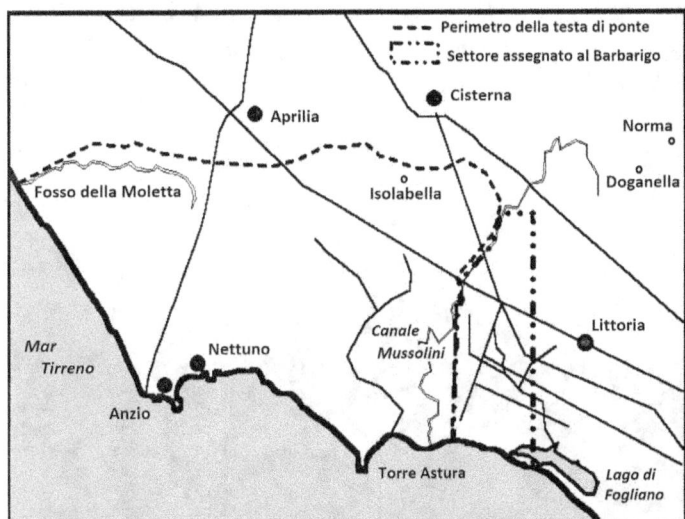

**The bridgehead with the sector assigned to the *Barbarigo*.**

**Marò of the *Barbarigo*.**

**Nettuno Front, March 1944: a defensive position of the 'Barbarigo'.**

The division had suffered heavy losses since the beginning and for this purpose, *Oberst* von Schellerer expressed to Bardelli his intention to use the Marò of the *Barbarigo* to reinforce his decimated companies. But the Italian commander opposed that proposal, maintaining that the *Barbarigo* was an organic unit formed of Italian soldiers and all his men, from officers to sailors, were determined to fight under the Italian flag and for the Italian cause and no one would agree to be integrated in German units. The battalion had to fight united, while still being tactically dependent on a German unit. In this regard, let us listen to the testimony of Lieutenant Giulio Cencetti: "... *And Bardelli begins to speak: staccato, quick ... The German* [von Schellerer]*, does not understand, but understands that he has an Italian different from those who described him ... Lieutenant Rattazzi began to translate .. 'this unit was born to fight as a cohesive unit ... It, made up of Italian volunteers with Italian flag, with Italian uniforms and weapons, commanded by Italian officers, claims its own sector well assigned in the deployment, which it responsible for and for which it will fight to the last marine. The 'Barbarigo' will never be reserve unit which is made up of animal handlers. We will continue to fight, we are not going to suffer any strange "cobelligerency". ... It's fine. Agreed. A company to the Mussolini Canal in all haste, because there is a need for men there. Another two deployed along the shore of Lago di Fogliano, through Strada Nascosta, for the Strada Lunga, up to the Gorgolicino ditch. A fourth in Sezze, undergoing a quick training update on German equipment, and as the situation allows the other companies will be pulled from the line to go to Sezze ...* ".

**The village of Littoria and the Lepini Mountains seen from the positions of the *Barbarigo*.**

**Marines of the *Barbarigo* on the Anzio front, 1944.**

After heated talks, von Schellerer then accepted Bardelli's requests: the four companies would be deployed along the *Grenadier-Regiment 735* sector, from the section of the Mussolini Canal towards the sea to Borgo Piave, Cerreto Alto and Borgo Sabotino. Immediately after establishing themselves on the front line, the individual companies took turns in training courses with German instructors, above all to instruct the marines to use the main anti-tank weapons, such as the *Panzerfaust*. At the same time, the first casualties were recorded, during the first patrol actions and in the defensive fighting:

after the two German counter-offensives of the previous months, the front appeared completely static and recalled the struggle of the trenches of the First World War. The marshy terrain also made it impossible to dig deep holes in order to better shelter better from enemy fire. There was not a continuous defensive line either side, so it was easy for the patrols to easily infiltrate the enemy positions.

German defensive position with an 88 mm antiaircraft gun, March 1944.

Lieutenant Giulio Cencetti.

Let us listen again to the testimony of the Lieutenant Giulio Cencetti: "... the 1st Company approaches the Canale Mussolini: the empty foxholes are reached amidst the muffled swearing of the German guides 'Zutt" ... .'Ja. Italiener? Gut!' whispered the Krauts: 'Tommies here, a lot of boom boom'. 'Unsere Kompanie alles Kaputt' [our company, all of them dead.] But those unfortunate beggars, just because they were holding their submachine guns and four 8mm Bredas, were smiling, as if to say: "OK, we're here now. Yep, us, who know what we are!" In short, the Ia has relaxed .... For those who have not experienced it, perhaps cannot realize what it means, under the artillery fire of an entire enemy sector that for days has bracketed your positions, with an opponent who is facing you, at a distance separated only by a narrow stream... .The dawn appears gray, misty and overcast, just broken by the disc of a pale sun. On his first day at the front. Alberto Spagna (nineteen years old) wanted to see the line, that line which he had finally reached, on from La

*Spezia with his battalion ... He rises, the helmet rises above the edge of the foxhole, Alberto touches slender blades of grass that bend under his breath. In a moment his eyes see a whole dewy countryside, past the opposite bank ... A shot rings out. His eardrums ring with the sound like a bell from the pierced helmet. Nothing more. Rhe rolls down into the arms of his comrades ... He's the first one to die. Firing resumes along the front. Days of hell. Probes, attacks. Grenades, bursts of firing, screams coming, muzzle flashes going ... ".*

**Enzo Grossi.**

## Notes

(1) Born in Livorno on March 11, 1908, Umberto Bardelli after attending primary school, on October 18, 1924 he entered the Royal Naval Academy of Livorno as a Cadet Officer. At the beginning of the war, Bardelli found himself on board the minelayer submarine Zoea, engaged in missions to transport ammunition to Italian North Africa and laying mines. He then was assigned to the submarine Benedetto Brin and on October 25th, he passed through the Strait of Gibraltar submerged to reach the Atlantic base of Bordeaux. In February 1941, he embarked as chief engineer on the Reginaldo Giuliani, which in March moved to the German base of Gotenhafen. In February 1942, he returned to Italy, assigned to the office responsible for fitting out submarines in Taranto. Promoted to Major of Naval Engineers on October 18, 1942, he embarked on the battleship Vittorio Veneto. Decorated with the Military War Cross for Valor, between 22 May and 31 August 1943, he was embarked on the light cruiser Scipione Africano, participating in the forcing of the Strait of Messina (Operation Scilla) against the Anglo-American light units that were patrolling the area following the operations in Sicily in July 1943. Immediately after September 8, 1943, he reached Trieste, where he made himself available to the German military authorities, and then moved to Pula. As soon as he learned that Commander Borghese was reorganizing the Xª MAS Flotilla under the insignia of the Italian Social Republic, he left Trieste to reach the Muggiano barracks in La Spezia.

(2) Enzo Grossi was born in San Epigma, Brazil, on April 20, 1908. During the Second World War, he was in command of the submarines Medusa and Barbarigo. With the latter, he attacked and destroyed a Maryland-class battleship on May 20, 1942, while on October 6, 1942, he attacked and sank a Mississippi-class battleship. For these sinkings he was promoted and decorated with two gold medals for military valor by the Italian government and awarded with honors by the German government. After September 8, 1943, he joined the Italian Social Republic, taking command of the Betasom base in Bordeaux.

(3) Information obtained from Giorgio Pisanò, *"Gli ultimi in grigioverde"* (*"The last of those in grey-green"*), pages 1072, 1073.

## Bibliography

Mario Bordogna, *"Junio Valerio Borghese e la Xª Flottiglia MAS"*, Mursia, Milano, 2007

Guido Bonvicini, *"Decima Marinai! Decima Comandante!"*, Mursia, Milano

Daniele Lembo, *"I fantasmi di Nettunia"*, Edizioni Settimo Sigillo

Marino Perissinotto, *"Duri a morire - storia del Battaglione Barbarigo"*, Ermanno Albertelli

Perissinotto, Panzarasa, *"Come la Fenice"*, Editoriale Lupo

Giorgio Pisanò, *"Gli ultimi in grigioverde"*, C.D.L. Edizioni

# The Feder Files
## Short Biographies of Five non-German Waffen-SS war reporters
### by Marc Rikmenspoel

Leon Hobe.

Björn Björnsson.

**Kurt Feder** was a *Waffen-SS* war reporter photographer. His known photos were taken in Germany, away from the frontlines. Between late April and early June, 1944, Feder visited a camp that was hosting get togethers of German and non-German *Waffen-SS* war reporters. Since many of these reporters were experienced in serving near the front, this may have been an opportunity for the sharing of methods and techniques, for the benefit of those new to the role. Feder took photos of many of these reporters, and some non-German individuals have been identified. The following photos are all from the Feder contact sheets at the US National Archives. They have been digitally enhanced for this article by Remy Spezzano.

**Leon Hobe** was a Walloon photographer. Born on November 27, 1919, his father was a Rexist official, and Leon also joined the movement. He was one of the original batch of volunteers for the Legion Wallonie in 1941, which is shown by his ribbon for the Eastern Front Medal. Hobe's other insignia include an Edelweiss arm patch, for having served with the Legion Wallonie in the Caucasus campaign, the Formations du Combat badge of the Rexist militia, and the small rectangular badge of pre-war Rexist members. Within a few weeks of this photo being taken, Hobe was assigned to cover the Hitlerjugend Division in Normandy. He went missing in action at this assignment during June, 1944.

**Björn Björnsson** was born on October 15, 1909 in Iceland, which was then an autonomous part of Denmark. He was the son of Sveinn Björnsson, a leading Icelandic politician who became the first President of independent Iceland in 1944. Björn Björnsson was in Germany in the early part of World War 2, and enlisted in the *Waffen-SS* during October 1941. After basic training and time with a replacement unit, he served with Wiking during the division's 1942 campaigns between February 23 and September 22. He may have already been a war reporter during this time, though his file lists him as SS-Panzergrenadier. Björnsson earned the Panzer Assault Badge in Bronze, which he isn't wearing in this photo. Björnsson then was assigned to attend the 9th Shortened Wartime Course at the Junkerschule Bad Tölz. He failed to graduate, but was kept at the facility to attend the following 2nd Course for Germanic Officers. While one part of his file indicates that Björnsson was promoted to Untersturmführer on April 20, 1944, the photo included here shows he was still a Standartenoberjunker in May. He actually received his officer promotion on June 21, 1944, and was granted seniority from April 20, 1944. Björnsson spent the remainder of the war running the Waffen-SS press office in Copenhagen. His father had been born in that city, and the Björn had probably been there during his life. Icelandics of that era learned Danish in school, so he was an ideal candidate for his post. Björn Björnsson was arrested by Danish authorities at the end of the war. With Iceland now independent of Denmark, and his father the president, he was released after a year and sent to Iceland. He died on April 14, 1998.

Sam Gösta Borg.

**Sam Gösta Borg**, one of the first Swedes to volunteer for the Waffen-SS, and a Winter War veteran. Born on August 15, 1915, and a long-time National Socialist, Gösta Borg left his post with the Svea Lifeguards of the Swedish Army upon hearing of the German invasion of the Soviet Union. Borg and his Svea Lifeguards comrade Rarnar Linner crossed the border into Norway, and volunteered for *Waffen-SS* service. As experienced soldiers, the pair required minimal training. They reached the front during August, 1941, serving as infantrymen with Regiment *Westland*. Linner was particularly displeased with life in the *Waffen-SS*. Borg's opinion has not been recorded, but the pair applied for discharge, and this was granted on October 12, 1941, after they had served two months at the front. Back in Sweden, Borg and Linner rejoined the Svea Lifeguards, after first being briefly incarcerated for desertion. Borg soon missed his time in the *Waffen-SS*, but hoped his experience would allow him to become an officer in the Swedish Army. He successfully passed a qualifying course, but was informed he could only be accepted as an officer cadet if he signed a statement renouncing his National Socialist beliefs. Borg refused to this, and decided to instead reenlist in the *Waffen-SS*. During September 1943, Borg encountered Heino Meyer, another Swedish veteran of *Wiking*. Meyer had been discharged from the *Waffen-SS* after being badly wounded. He and Borg decided to reenlist together, and crossed the border to

Norway, where they signed their enlistment papers on October 2. Just over two weeks later, they began studying at Bad Tölz as part of the 3rd Course for Germanic Officers. Borg graduated on March 10, 1944, and received a direct promotion to *Untersturmführer* on that day. After initial plans to make him a combat officer, he was instead sent to Narva to join countrymen Carl Svensson, Hans-Caspar Kreuger, and Torkel Tillman as war reporters. This many reporters weren't needed together, so Borg and Tillman were soon on to new assignments. They first stopped at the German camp where the photos in this piece were taken. Borg next traveled to Finland, where the Soviet offensive that opened on June 9 in the Karelian Isthmus resulted in the largest battles ever fought in northern Europe, culminating in the Battle of Tali-Ihantala. Borg reported on this struggle for several weeks. Once the Finnish front settled down, Borg was sent to Poland, to cover the defensive battles of the IV. SS-Panzerkorps northeast of Warsaw. He then reported on the Warsaw Uprising, and photographed the final surrender of Polish commander Bor-Komorowski. Borg then headed west, covering the Battle of the Bulge. Once it failed, he was assigned to a radio station in Norway, to make propaganda broadcasts. Borg was discharged from the Waffen-SS in the last days of the war. He married his girlfriend, and returned to Sweden with her. He wrote a book about how Sweden could defend itself against a Soviet invasion, but was not permitted to rejoin the Swedish army. He died on December 29, 2000.

**Hans-Caspar Kreuger.**

**Hans-Caspar Kreuger** was the best-known Swedish war reporter. He was born on October 5, 1902, and was already 40 when he joined the *Waffen-SS* during 1942. He was a Swedish army veteran, who wore his badges from that service on his *Waffen-SS* uniform. Kreuger began as a simple soldier. A National Socialist, he wrote articles for the newspaper of the SSS Party, while serving with *Wiking*. This led to his reassignment to become an official war reporter. Kreuger remained with Wiking through the February 1944 Cherkassy breakout. He was then sent to Narva as an officer candidate. Kreuger took photographs of the soldiers fighting in the Narva area, and interviewed Dutch Knight's Cross winner Gerardes Mooyman, who arrived at the Nederland Brigade during April. Kreuger left the front during May, to attend the gathering shown in this piece's photo. He was promoted to

*Untersturmführer* on June 21, 1944. By this time, Kreuger was back at Narva, but his service was soon suspended. He had been accused of molesting male soldiers, so SS authorities launched an investigation. Swedish combat officer Hans-Gösta Pehrsson encouraged Kreuger to shoot himself. Freitod, honorable suicide, was the end for many SS men suspected of homosexual activity. Kreuger insisted on defending himself. The investigation eventually concluded that Kreuger was not truly homosexual. Instead, he lost control of his actions when under the influence of alcohol. Kreuger was required to abstain from consuming alcohol, and was allowed to return to service. In the meantime, Kreuger had been hospitalized in Vienna, due to sickness. He acquired an apartment there, possibly during this treatment. By early 1945, Kreuger was commanding the War Reporters Platoon of the *Nordland* Division. He led his men through the 1945 fighting in Pomerania, and across the Oder. When the German front began disintegrating during the Soviet Berlin Offensive, starting on April 16, Kreuger made sure his platoon was out of the fighting. They marched west toward American captivity, with Kreuger then heading south to his apartment in Vienna. He seems to have managed to hide his *Waffen-SS* membership, perhaps pretending to be merely a Swedish citizen caught up in the events of the end of the war. Kreuger eventually made his way to Argentina, where he served as an advisor to the Argentinian Army, and lived until his death on August 15, 1977.

**Carl-Johannes Herman Thorkell Tillmann.**

Carl-Johannes Herman Thorkell Tillmann was born in Sweden on November 19, 1917, to a Swedish father and a German mother. His parents divorced during his childhood, so Thorkell Tillmann spent a few years with a foster family in Germany. During this time, he was a member of the Hitler Youth. This is reflected in the included photo, which shows Tillmann wearing the Hitler Youth Honor Badge next to a sports badge. Tillmann returned to Sweden in 1934, and became a soldier, serving as an NCO. After being accused of espionage, for which no evidence was produced, he came to Germany in the spring of 1942, and soon joined the *Waffen-SS*. As an NCO of long experience, Tillmann then served as an instructor at the Germanic House in Sennheim, Alsace. He was selected for officer training, and attended the 11.

Shortened Wartime Course at Bad Tölz. After graduation, Tillmann was sent with Gösta Borg to Narva, as a war reporter. Possibly due to his background as a Hitler Youth member, Tillmann was sent to Normandy during June, 1944, to cover the *Hitlerjugend* Division. With that unit he was killed in action near Cheux on June 26, during the British Goodwood offensive. Tillmann had been promoted to *Untersturmführer* five days earlier. He left behind a wife, and a daughter born in May 1943.

Kreuger was also photographed in two sequences of group photos. He is on the right in both of these images. The other war reporters with him, have, so far, not been identified.

## Bibliography

Bouysse, Gregory, "*Encyclopedie de L'Ordre Nouveau – Wallonie Partie II*", Self-published 2018.

Larsson, Lars T., "*Hitler's Swedes*", Helion & Co., Solihull, UK, 2015.

Moore, John P., "*Führerliste der Waffen-SS*", JP Moore Publishing, Portland, Oregon, 2003.

**Special thanks to Remy Spezzano for his generous effort to make the photos look their best.**

# The battle for Carentan: June 1944
by Massimiliano Afiero

'GbV' grenadiers marching towards the front lines, June 1944.

During the morning of 12 June, some elements of 6./37 led by SS-Ostuf. Teetzmann reached the area south of Carentan; during the afternoon the commander of II./37, SS-Stubaf. Opificius, also arrived with elements of the 9./37. The 6/37 was ordered to reinforce Ostbataillon 439, composed of Ukrainian volunteers commanded by Hauptmann Hans Becker, that was located on Hill 30. While they were on the march, the SS grenadiers encountered army infantrymen and paratroopers who told them:" We're all that's left". "And what about the Eastern vounteers?" asked Teetzmann. "They disappeared" was the reply. The grenadiers continued to advance along the national route, encountering nests of American resistance and tanks. Following brief firefights, Teetzmann's men along with a few German paratroopers, tried to reach Hill 30, no longer from the east but rather from the west. The maneuver was forestalled with the Germans being subjected to a hellish amount of enemy fire, and finally having to abandon the attack. Around 22:00 the bulk of his 6.Kompanie reached the positions defended by von der Heydte's paratroopers. Another one of the division's units that was engaged on 12 June, was 1./SS-Pz.Gr.Rgt.37 led by SS-Hstuf. Wilhelm Schlebes[1] who had been ordered to retake the village of Auvers, occupied by American paratroopers. SS-Stubaf. Christian Reinhardt[2], his battalion commander, said "…Your company will be enough". The 2nd Platoon led by SS-Oscha. Schrag took the lead; the NCO moved out far ahead of his men, and once fighting began with the Americans, all trace of him was lost. When his grenadiers advanced under the cover of a small hill, they found Schrag's lifeless body in the grass. The grenadiers of the 1st Platoon led by *SS-Ustuf*. Heinz Streck moved forward and were able to take the small hil and enter the village of Auvers. Not all of the American paratroopers were able to disengage in time, and many were thus taken prisoner. The company's heavy machine guns were set up in the church belfry and reconnaissance patrols were sent out in the surrounding area.

*Waffen SS* grenadiers and *Luftwaffe* paratroopers marching towards the front line.

A *5.Kp./SS-Pz.Gr.Rgt.38* motorcycle and sidecar in Normandy, June 1944.

*SS-Hstuf.* Schlebes soon informed the battalion headquarters that he had established control over Auvers and its surroundings. Shortly afterwards his company was relieved by *2.Kompanie* commanded by *SS-Ostuf.* Fritz von Boeckmann[3]. While awaiting the arrival to the area of other units of the division, it was up to the paratroopers to defend the front line from which the counterattack against Carentan was to be mounted. Meanwhile preparations continued at a fever pitch: the heavy weapons were to take up positions south of the road near the village of Baupte, protected by the *14.(Flak)/37 Kompanie* under *SS-Hstuf.* von Seebach[4]. Of the sixty gas-powered trucks under *SS-Ustuf.* Hutt[5] that carried the ninety tons of ammunition for the division, only fifteen reached their destination because of the defection of their French drivers and destruction by Allied air attacks. That same morning of 12 June, *Oberleutnant* Pöppel of 12./FJR.6, was sent to headquarters of the *Generalkommando LXXIV.Armee-Korps* at Saint-Lô; after having reported on the situation, he requested that his regiment be put under the orders of the *GvB*, rather than under the *91.Luftlande Division*, for logistical support reasons. The chief of staff of the *LXXXIV.Armee-Korps*, *Oberstleutnant* von Criegern, confirmed the transfer of *FJR 6* to *GvB* control. At the same time that *Oberleutnant* Pöppel assumed command of the regiment near Raffoville, *General der Artillerie* Marcks was mortally wounded during an Allied air attack in the Caumont sector.

*SS-Brigadeführer* **Ostendorff.**

## Preparations for the attack

During the evening of 12 June, *SS-Brigadeführer* Ostendorff and *SS-Stubaf.* Conrad put together the final details of the attack plan for 13 June, whose objective was to recapture Carentan, drafting the following order for the division:

*"1) Enemy forces between the Orne and Vire rivers, probably reinforced by a new American army corps with the intention of continuing to advance to the south. At the same time, the enemy is attempting to enlarge his landing area at Saint Mère-Eglise in order to cut off the Cherbourg peninsula with the previously mentioned forces. Carentan is occupied by elements of the 101st Airborne Division. We can expect the employment of tanks and intervention of powerful naval gunfire. The American fighting methods are crafty and astute. Nasty combat spirit. The enemy uses phosphorous shells fired by their artillery that cause serious burns and employs artificial fog with an effect similar to that of tear gas. Use gas masks immediatey!*

*2) The GvB SS-Panzer-Grenadier-Division, with Kampfgruppe Heintz (Author's note: of the 275.Inf.Div., commanded by Oberst Heintz) and Fallschirmjäger-Regiment 6…, will defend the western bank of the River Vire and will retake Carentan…*

**Paratroopers from *Fallschirmjäger-Regiment 6* in Normandy, June 1944.**

*4) Kampfgruppe Heintz will defend the current sector, will hold the main line of resistance and impede enemy penetrations coming from the north and from the other side of the St.Pellerin-Carentan railway line and from east of the other side of the River Vire. The enemy must be attacked, even by night, with intense activity by assault troops.*

*5) SS-Panzer-Grenadier-Regiment 38 will assemble in the area of Mesnil-Angot-Rauline-St.Fromond-St.Jean de*

*Daye-La Goucherie and will establish intervention groups to immediately repel with counterattacks any enemy that might break through the main line of resistance.*

*6) Following the capture of Carentan by* SS-Panzer-Grenadier-Regiment 37, Fallschirmjäger-Regiment 6 *will occupy the re-established main line of resistance and will hold it. During the course of the attack by* SS-Panzer-Grenadier-Regiment 37, *the northern flank must be covered along the line Pommenauque-Aussaie. A battalion must follow up the attack, echeloned in depth in order to keep the rear area free in the event of any surprises (airborne landings)....*

A defensive position with a *Panzerschreck* and hand grenades in Normandy, Summer 1944.

SS grenadiers armed with Mauser rifles, waiting for the enemy, June 1944.

*Fallschirmjäger* on a defensive position, June 1944.

*Fallschirmjäger* armed with a *Panzerfaust*, June 1944.

*8)* SS-Panzer-Grenadier-Regiment 37, *reinforced by a company from SS-Pz.Abt.17 and a platoon of Sf-Kp/SS-Pz.Jg.Abt.17 will establish positions south and north of Domville during the night between 12 and 13 June, ir order to be able to attack to the east, beginning to march at 5:20, ensuring control of the area west of Carentan (south of the Carentan-Baupte railway line) and will capture the city. In the event of a favorable outcome, you will continue to the north as far as the Moulin-St.Côme line and establish a bridgehead. To that end, enough forces must be available that will be able, once the city has been captured, to immediately pursue the enemy...*

*10) The following units are placed under command of the* Kommandeur *of SS-Art.Rgt.17:*

*- the "Ernst" artillery group, led by SS-Hstuf. Ernst, commander of I./SS-*

A 20mm *Flakvierling* **mounted on a half-track.**

Art.Rgt.17
- II.Art.Rgt.191 *of the* 91.Luftlande-Division
- 2 s.F.H. Batterien *of the* 352.Inf.Div...

*11)* Luftwaffe *support: support for the division's attack is planned as follows:*
*a- prior to the beginning of the attack, by a bomber formation*
*b- once the attack has begun, by attack aircraft in front of the positions involved in the attack".*

## The counterattack begins

At 5:30 on 13 June, with the countryside heavy with morning mist, the preparatory artillery fire began, while the grenadiers of *SS-Pz.Gr.Rgt.37* waited for the signal to move out on the attack. At 5:45 the assault guns of *1.* and *2./SS-Pz.Abt.17* followed the grenadiers when they fired red flares in the air to alert the artillery to lengthen its fire. The heavy weapons of *SS-Pz.Gr.Rgt.37*, which had not arrived until late in the night on 12 June, were emplaced south of the road to Baupte, very close to each other. They were protected by *14.(Flak)37* under *SS-Hstuf.* Hans von Seebach, while *6./37* had remained in the rear, along the Baupte road, as a reserve company.

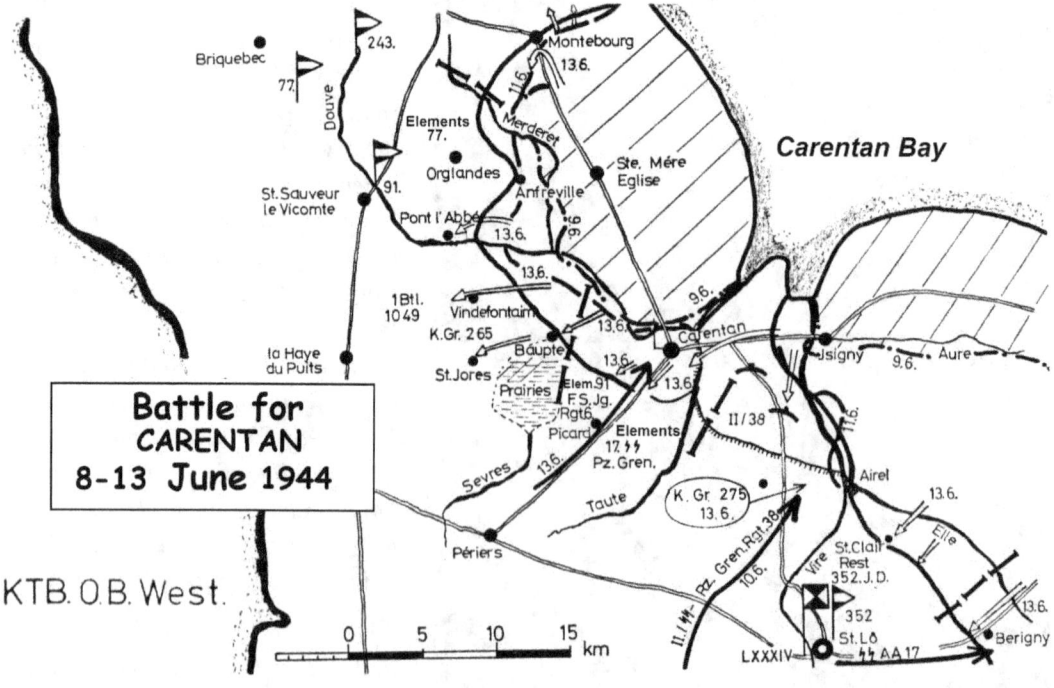

**Battle for CARENTAN 8-13 June 1944**

*Carentan Bay*

KTB. O.B. West.

The command posts of *SS-Pz.Gr.Rgt.37* and *of II./37* had been set up near Cantepie, two kilometers east of Auvers, where the command post of *Fallschirmjäger-Regiment 6* was also located. During the previous night, advanced patrols had been able to open gaps in the minefields that had been laid by the enemy. The attack initially went well, but then when the companies crossed the Carentan-Douville road they came under enemy fire, suffering their first losses: many soldiers fell mortally wounded from shots to the head from accurate sniper fire. When the morning mist began to lift, snipers hidden in trees were quickly spotted, paratroopers from the 101st Airborne Division. The *Flak-Zug* of *SS-Pz.Abt.17*, led by *SS-Hscha*. Dornacher, then entered in action with its three four-barreled 20 mm guns, shredding all of the surrounding vegetation in order to hit the enemy snipers. Once that threat had been eliminated, the attack resumed. *SS-Hstuf*. Schlebes advanced at the head of his *1.Kompanie*. Shortly afterwards the battalion's other two companies, the 2nd and the 3rd, were also in the thick of the fighting.

An SS grenadier advancing under enemy fire.

German soldiers under fire.

German soldiers of the 17th SS withdraw after a battle near Carentan, June 1944.

The heavy machine guns and mortars of *4.Kompanie* provided adequate supporting fire to the attacking grenadiers. The American artillery in turn entered into action, sowing panic and terror amongst the SS units. After having silently crept up to the enemy positions, the SS grenadiers found themselves unexpectedly under enemy fire: the companies and platoons broke up into small groups, all seeking to find some kind of shelter. *SS-Ostuf.* von Boeckmann took it upon himself to rally the men, collecting some isolated personnel of the heavy platoon of *1.Kompanie* as well as several paratroopers. Other small combat groups were scratched together in the field. *SS-Ostuf*. Helmuth Wagner[6], commander of *3.Kompanie*, also rallied many lost soldiers around him, throwing them into an attack against enemy positions. Allied heavy artillery came to the support of the defenders of Carentan along with naval gunfire offshore. The German forward elements soon found themselves cut off and surrounded and about to be completely wiped out. Some American units counterattacked, while other units defending the city held on doggedly.

**Carentan sector: an aid station in the swamp area with GvB soldiers and *Fallschirmjäger*.**

**GvB soldiers and *Fallschirmjäger* between the rubble of the train station in Carentan.**

The attack by the SS grenadiers and the German paratroopers had been stopped cold near the railway station a few hundred meters before the first houses in Carentan. At 7:31 an initial report was sent by the *I./37*: "*...the advance is proceeding despite strong enemy resistance. The Americans are pulling back... Some enemy groups are still in our attack sector. Our losses are moderately high*". Around 9:00, the *I./37* reached the southeastern limits of Carentan and shortly afterwards the *II./6* led by *Hauptmann* Mager, reached the city's railway station. At the same time a report was received from the left wing, where the *III./6* was fighting: the outskirts of Carentan had been reached. Some strong enemy groups, however, were still putting up resistance. Artillery fire against Carentan was requested, as sounds of approaching tanks began to be heard. At 9:15, the right wing reported that it would not be possible to eliminate enemy resistance without the support of tanks. By 9:00, the units had been able to advance only five hundred meters. At 9:50, the I./37 reported that it had ceased its attack against the city. At that same moment the American 2nd Armored Division attacked with tanks. At 10:45, the I./37, under strong enemy pressure, was forced to withdraw.

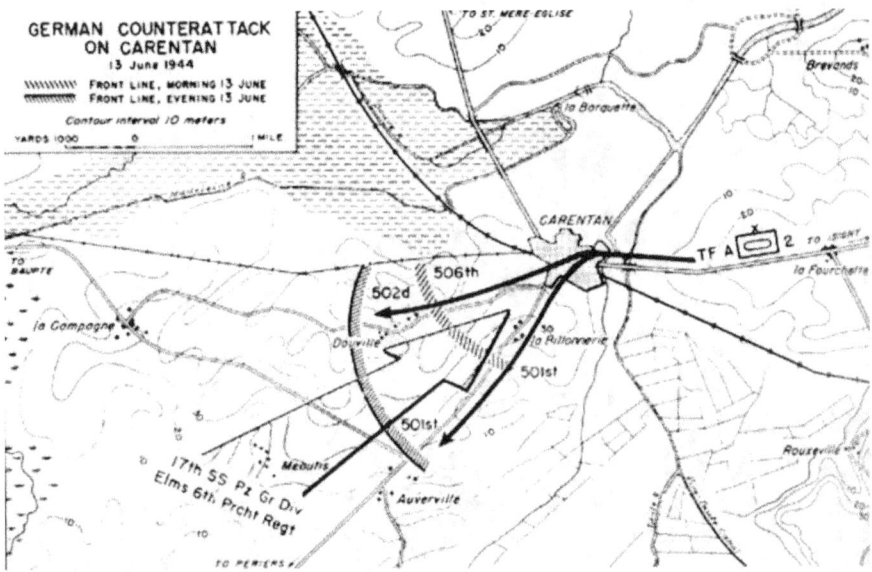

In the meantime, 6./37 had been ordered to advance; after having covered about 800 meters, on the outskirts of a village the company ran across the paratroopers that had withdrawn from Carentan. SS-Ostuf. Teetzmann deployed his men in a semi-circle around the village of La Mare des Pierres, northeast of Méautis, and was shortly thereafter attacked by the Americans. A 75 mm Pak of 8.(schw.)/37 that had been emplaced was knocked out and overrun by American tanks after having fired a few rounds. The American units bypassed the village and continued their attack to the southeast.

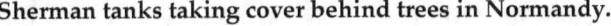

**Sherman tanks taking cover behind trees in Normandy.**     **American infantrymen.**

At 10:30, American tanks began to engage the StuG of GvB, while at the same time, with the help of their artillery, pushing back the SS grenadiers. The GvB assault guns were able to knock out several American tanks, but once again numerical superiority favored the enemy. The SS grenadiers began to fall back along with the assault guns, despite the fact that *SS-Ostubaf.* Fick had ordered that the positions be held at all costs. A platoon from *2.Kompanie*, led by *SS-Ustuf.* Samek[7], had been completely surrounded and it was due only to the providential arrival of an assault gun that it managed to withdraw.

Grenadiers of *3.Kp./SS-Pz.Gr.Rgt.38* withdrawing following an attack against enemy positions southwest of Carentan (*Stöber collection*).

*Waffen SS* grenadiers in an assault, Normandy 1944.

Most of the forces that had taken part in the assault on Carentan, as mentioned previously, ended up scattered in small groups. Among them was a group led by *SS-Rottenführer* Hoffmann of *1.Kompanie*, who had been ordered to create a diversion to allow the other groups to withdraw; during a firefight with the Americans, Hoffmann's group was subjected to bazooka fire ant the *Rottenführer* himself was gravely wounded. At 14:00, the general attack kicked off with tanks and the 501st Parachute Infantry Regiment of the 101st Airborne Division. At that point, the German counterattack could be considered to have been definitively ended, also in view of the massive intervention by Allied air power.

SS grenadiers in a defensive position.

A photo of two destroyed *StuG.IV* on RN 171.

A *'GvB' StuG.IV*, Normandy 1944.

# Withdrawal

*SS-Brigdf.* Ostendorff was thus forced to call his troops back to their departure points. The withdrawal of the units took place without being subjected to too much enemy pressure, but along *RN 171* two *Sturmgeschütz* of *I./Zug* of *1./SS-Pz.Abt.17* were knocked out. A new defensive line was then established five hundred meters north of the swamps at Balerie, five hundred meters south of the village of Meauty, along *RN 171* as far as the fork with *Route Nationale 971* near Auerville, a thousand meters north of St.Quentin as far as the flooded area of the River Taute. In the early afternoon, the *6./37* also pulled back to the new main line of resistance. In its battalion sector, the *II./37* shifted to the east of RN 171 up to the flooded area, positioned as the middle company. The *I./37* dug in to the left of the road. To its left, *Fallschirmjäger-Regiment 6* took up positions that reached up to the edge of the swamp, with *Ost-Bataillon 635* under its command. *SS-Brigdf.* Ostendorff set up his command post at Saint-Sébastien-de-Raids, east of Périers, while the command post of *SS-Pz.Gr.Rgt.37* was established near Neuville and that of *Fallschirmjäger-Regiment 6* near Raffoville.

The failure of the German counterattack was due mainly to the shortage of men and equipment: *Luftwaffe* support was limited to an attack by only two aircraft, which were unable to provide any meaningful support to the attacking ground forces.

On their side, the Allies were able to count on a huge array of heavy weapons, artillery and tanks. In order to counter the armor threat, the Germans were able to field only one *Panzerjäger* platoon of *3./SS-Pz.Jg.Abt.17* and a single company of *StuG IV* assault guns. For close-in anti-tank defense, there was a lack of effective weapons such as the *Panzerfaust* and the *Ofenrohr* (*Panzerschreck*). When the *GvB* elements were stalled on the western outskirts of Carentan, the Americans launched an attack along the Carentan-Périers stretch of *RN 171*. On the northern side of Carentan, Hill 30, occupied by *Ost-Bataillon 439*, was abandoned following the death of its commander, *Hauptmann* Becker. The Americans were thus able to continue their advance unmolested. During the evening, the *GvB* organized a new defensive line south of Carentan as far as the swamp at Gorges. The fighting for Carentan and the pocket created near Baupte and north of that location had "mixed" the units that were committed, obliging *LXXXIV.Armee-Korps* to order a new defensive arrangement.

## New counterattacks

On the morning of 14 June, units of the 101st Airborne Division launched an attack along the Carentan-Périers road, but were stopped near the localities of Picard and Sadoterie, where they ran into

**A series of photos showing *SS-Stubaf.* Fick while leading his men in the fighting south of Carentan.**

positions held by *II./SS-Pz.Gr.Rgt.37* under *SS-Stubaf.* Hans Opificius, and in particular against the positions defended by the remnants of *6.Kompanie*. Allied artillery as well as aviation hit the German positions very heavily, which were in danger of being overrun from one minute to the next. At that point, *SS-Ostuf.* Teetzmann, commander of *6./SS-Pz.Gr.Rgt.37*, made the only decision possible in an attempt to re-stabilize the situation: counterattack! Out of sheer desperation, and motivated by admirable courage, the SS grenadiers left their burrows to attack the enemy; the ground that had been lost was quickly retaken and the defensive front held by *II./37* became quiet again.

Grenadiers from *GvB* armed with hand grenades and heavy weapons in the Carentan area.

A *StuG.IV* of *SS-Pz.Abt.17* destroyed on 13 June in the area southwest of Carentan. While attempting to exit the vehicle through the upper hatch, its commander was killed.

The devastating effect of Allied air power in Normandy: destroyed tanks and ambulances.

The situation in which *I./37*, led by *SS-Stubaf.* Reinhardt, found itself, appeared equally dramatic: the paratroopers who had been on his left flank had pulled back, leaving the positions in the hands of the Americans, who soon attacked. *SS-Ostubaf.* Fick had no other reserves and his *III./37* was still en route on bicycles. He was thus forced to send into the front line his headquarters staff, including drivers, telephone operators, secretaries, medical personnel and anyone else who was able to hold and use a weapon. Armed with rifles, submachine guns and a few hand grenades, the improvised combatants threw themselves into a furious and dramatic counterattack, and for many of them it was their baptism of fire. With the fighting under way, the fate of the division's several hundred wounded personnel who had already been sent to aid stations began to become tragic; the wounded soldiers were moved to the castle at Savigny or to the abbey at Hambye, while the most seriously wounded were moved to Le Mans. Moving along the roads was, however, always a daunting undertaking: on 14 June, a terrible tragedy took place on the road between Saint-Sauveur and Marigny, when a convoy bearing wounded soldiers from the division was attacked by Allied fighter-bombers. Six large buses, with red crosses painted on their roofs, caught fire. The few survivors who were able to throw themselves into the ditch alongside the road before the explosions were witness to a terrible spectacle, finding charred corpses everywhere.

**Normandy 1944: a German convoy caught in the open by Allied air forces, with devastating human losses.**

*SS-Oscha.* **Ewald Scheidt of the** *SS-Pz.A.A.17.*

*Sturmmann* **Beinert of the 4.Kp./SS-Pz.A.A.17.**

The men of the *GvB* reconnaissance detachment reached the scene of the tragedy shortly after the Allied aircraft had left and found only a very few survivors, mainly nurses, who had had the good fortune to have abandoned the vehicles in time. The SS scouts could not tarry; after having fought to the east, along the edge of the forest of Balleroi, they had been ordered to move to the central sector of the Cotentin peninsula, in the area of Saint-Sauver-le-Vicomte. While crossing through the hamlet of Saint-Auver-Landelin, *2./SS-Aufkl.-Abt.17*, under *SS-Ustuf.* Günther, was attacked by allied aircraft before reaching Périers. The recon personnel quickly jumped to the ground, seeking shelter, abandoning their *Schwimmwagen* vehicles. Their losses were minimal, but were more serious for *3.* and *4.Kompanie*. Once the position at Périers had been passed, the *GvB* reconnaissance group continued on to Saint-Jores, towards Saint-Sauver-le-Vicomte on 15 June.

**GvB grenadiers engaged in fighting on the Carentan front. (*Charles Trang Coll.*).**

**A pre-war photo of K.H. Nieschlag.**

*1.Kompanie* led by *SS-Ostuf.* Gerhard Arnken, with its armored cars, proceeded towards Raids, while *3.Kompanie* under *SS-Ostuf.* Albert Buck was sent to Neufmesnil to provide protection to the north. *2.Kompanie* under *SS-Ustuf.* Walzinger headed south of the swamp at Gorges, establishing defensive positions. *4.Kompanie* led by *SS-Ustuf.* Hans Mumm and *5.Kompanie* under *SS-Ostuf.* Helmut Prieler were tasked to occupy the area of Douville and Varanguebec, where the headquarters of the recon battalion was also set up. In this manner the left wing of the division was solidly reinforced, while the right wing was still in difficult straits in the area between the Taute and Vire rivers.

## The situation east of Carentan

During the attack against Carentan, other units of the *GvB* were engaged in defending the area to the east of the city, north of the Vire Canal, on the River Taute. These were the grenadiers of *II./SS-Pz.Gr.Rgt.38*, under *SS-Stubaf.* Karl-Heinz Nieschlag[8], supported by an assault gun company, the *3./SS-Pz.Abt.17*. On June 6, 1944, there was only one company of *Fallschirmjäger-Regiment 6* and *Ost-Bataillon 439* present in that sector. On 8 June, most of the German forces had withdrawn towards Isigny-sur-Mer, which was captured the following day by American forces. To slow down the enemy advance in that sector, *II./38*, which from 10 June had taken up positions along the Taute-Vire Canal, was sent to the area of La Tringale, nine kilometers east of Graignes. Also on 10 June, *I./SS-Pz.Gr.Rgt.38* under *SS-Hstuf.* Otto Ertel, along with *9./SS-Pz.Gr.Rgt.38* under *SS-Hstuf.* Krehnke, arrived to support Nieschlag's battalion. Most of these elements had made it to Normandy aboard civilian vehicles or on bicycles, but in all cases were not complete units. In the meantime the Americans had profited from this chaos to expand their bridgehead, firmly establishing themselves east of the Vire and Elle rivers. In an attempt to close the breach, the German command had sent as reinforcement a march battalion from the engineer school at Angers, the *Pionier Bataillon Angers* commanded by *Hauptmann* Schdeffold, to be employed as infantry, in support of the GvB units. During the ensuing fighting, the SS units suffered heavy losses, among them *SS-Hstuf.* Horst Rehtmeyer[9], commander of *8./SS-Pz.Gr.Rgt.38*, who fell in combat near St-Pellerin. In the afternoon, following a forced march, units of *II./SS-Pz.Gr.Rgt.38* reached St-Jean-de-Daye and the *5./38* continued along the *RN 171* as far as the canal. On 11 June, after the fighting at St-Pellerin, elements of *8./38* met up with groups from *5.* and *7./38* on the hill at Lenauderie, two kilometers northwest of Montmartin-en-Graignes. The leading patrol, under *SS-Uscha.* Böffert of the *5./38*, had advanced as far as Montseaux, to the left of *RN 174*, without running into the enemy, until it was stopped by American tanks and was forced to pull back.

**A group of GvB grenadiers lined up and armed to the teeth, with belts of linked cartridges and hand grenades, prior to an attack.**

To the right of RN 174, contact with *7./38* had meanwhile been established. In the morning, *5./38* resumed its march to the north to reach Briseval. The first clash with the Americans occurred around noontime. A patrol under *SS-Uscha.* Böffert was advancing at the head of the company while maintaining contact on the right with *7./38*. With his men, Böffert reached Rouxeville, where the French were celebrating the arrival of the Allies and their liberation! Turning back, at Montseaux, the patrol encountered an American tank which was quickly turned back after having been fired at by an 88 mm anti-tank gun belonging *to 8.38*. On 12 June, *II./38* was engaged against paratroopers of the 101st Airborne inside Graignes since dawn. The only reinforcement came from *2./Pi.Btl. Angers* and the only heavy weapons were those of *8.(schw.)/38*. The battalion headquarters and *8.38* were engaged on Hill 35 fending off enemy tanks, mainly by using grenades.

SS grenadiers on the watch for advancing enemy units.

SS grenadiers sheltering behind walls in a village of the Taute, June 1944.

American prisoners in Normandy, 1944.

That same day, two battalions of the U.S. 29th Infantry Division attacked Montmartin-en-Graignes, which had already been heavily shelled by naval gunfire, hitting the location. While *1./Pi.Btl. "Angers"* was providing cover on the right towards the Vire, *2./Pi.Btrl. "Angers"* under *Hauptmann* Neumann and elements of *II.38* to which the surviving elements of *Grenadier-Regiment 984* of *352.Inf.Div.* had attached themselves busied themselves in protecting the left sector. The American units were nevertheless able to bypass Montmartin to the east and advance along the Vire-Taute Canal. It became necessary to commit personnel of the headquarters of *III./38* to defend the *II./38* command post. During the day of 13 June the Americans were able to break through the German defenses and reach the Vire Canal along the Taute and *Route Nationale 174* that ran from Carentan to Saint-Lô. *SS-Stubaf.* Nieschlag sent two assault groups of *9./II./SS-Pz.Gr.38* on the counterattack, reinforced by non-combat personnel of his own headquarters staff. His orders were categorical: *"Liquidate the enemy breakthrough!"*. The two groups, one advancing on the right and one on the left, threw themselves into the attack, along the way gathering up several army troops who had been cut off. In one house they took about thirty prisoners and another thirty in a wooded area. The following is what *SS-Oberscharführer* Steimle had to say:" SS-Sturmbannrführer *Nieschlag ordered Schlegel and me to clear out the pocket. In addition to the staff personnel, there were two groups from* 9.Kp.*, Schlegel was on the left and I was on the right.*

A *Nebelwerfer* rocket launcher on the Normandy front, June 1944.

*Nebelwerfer* firing rockets at the enemy s position.

An American forward reconnaissance patrol.

*Schlegel soon made contact with the enemy in the hedges, and was killed in the fighting. I managed to flank the enemy on the right and from there, with the scattered Wehrmacht soldiers, reached an open field. We captured about thirty prisoners from one house. Around noontime the action was over. Making a sweep of the fields with two Americans in search of any wounded, we found a seriously wounded American who spoke perfect German. His mother had come from Schleswig-Holstein. During the night, we were once again engaged against a village, slightly to the right of our command post. After a short Nebelwerfer barrage we made our attack, but in the empty village we found only one dead person".*

On 15 June, elements of the U.S. 30th Infantry Division, who had relieved the U.S. 29th Infantry Division, launched an attack at 7:30, moving from the sector to the north of Carentan. Supported by five artillery groups, they advanced along the railway line and captured Lenauderie after fighting that lasted forty minutes. Then they reached Montmartin-en-Graignes, and after an hour of violent fighting, also captured it. Towards nightfall, the American units, supported by tanks, reached the village of La Raye, on the Vire and the Taute, with a battalion. But the bridge over the Vire had been blown. At the division headquarters, in Saint-Sébastien-de-Raids, the men were in a fever pitch.

A GvB *MG-42* in position, ready to fire (*Stöber Collection*).

American infantry in the *bocage*.

*SS-Brigadeführer* **Werner Ostendorff, on the right, conferring with other SS GvB officers.**

*SS-Stubaf.* Conrad reported to Ostendorff: *"It is now clear that the Americans are pushing to the west, in an attempt to reach the coast and to cut our forces in two. Our comrades to the north, who are surrounded, will inevitably be pushed back towards Cherbourg"*.

On the morning of the 16th, resistance at La Raye ceased, after which the canal was reached, where the Americans assumed a defensive position. On the same day they also gained ground to the west, reaching Douville. The few troops of *I./38* engaged in that sector crossed the canal and fell back in the area of Graignes. *SS-Oscha.* Becker of *8./38* was ordered to carry out a reconnaissance north of the last bridge on the Vire Canal still in German hands. The NCO crossed the canal around noontime, heading towards the castle of Briseval. South of Montmartin he ran across the last army stragglers who had been cut off. Ostendorff himself followed the recon party to determine personally the true situation on the front line, accompanied by only one officer. During the move towards the castle at Briseval, *SS-Brigdf.* Ostendorff crossed paths with an American jeep that was fleeing from the German lines. In the brief firefight that ensued, the *GvB* commander was seriously wounded in the head. Aided by *SS-Oscha*. Becker, he was quickly brought to the rear area and from there by ambulance to the hospital as Sées. *SS-Staf.* Binge, commander of the artillery regiment, assumed temporary command of the division. During the night between 16 and 17 June, *II./38, Kampfguppe Heintz* and *Pionier-Bataillon "Angers"* crossed to the southern bank of the Vire-Taute Canal.   *SS-Pz.Gr.Rgt.38*, whose command post was in the castle at Mesnil-Vencroire, assumed control of the sector that ran from St André de Bohon to RN 174.

**A destroyed vehicle belonging to *Stabs-Kp./SS-Pi.Btl.17*.**     *SS-Ostubaf.* Otto Binge.

*SS-Staf.* Otto Baum.

The new *GvB* defensive front, about thirty kilometers long, extended from the swampy area as far as the Vire. From left to right, the following units were engaged: *Fallschirmjäger-Regiment 6* with two battalions, *SS-Pz.Gr.Rgt.37* with three battalions, the *I./38, Pionier-Bataillon "Angers"*, *Kampfgruppe Heintz* and the *II./38*. For a few days the front quieted down and the Allies and Germans, short of breath, took advantage of it to reorganize their ranks. With the arrival of good weather, Allied aviation returned to strike the *GvB* positions, forcing the SS grenadiers to live like moles in their holes covered with shrubbery.

## A new commander: Otto Baum

On June 18, 1944 Field Marshal Rommel, commander of Army Group B, made a personal inspection visit to *LXXXIV.Armee-Korps*, noting that the forces defending the Cotentin peninsula, on the left wing of the invasion front, were short of men and equipment.  He thus promised to send in two armored divisions as quickly as possible, the *Panzer Lehr Division* under Bayerlein and the *Das Reich* under Lammerding. That same day, the new commander of the *GvB* , *SS-Staf.* Otto Baum[10], was designated. As soon as he arrived in Normandy,

Baum found himself facing a very critical situation. Not even on the horrible Eastern Front had he ever seen such enemy superiority in men and equipment. Reinforcements continued to pour in on the Normandy beaches without letup, while the German forces on the Cotentin peninsula were about to be cut in two. In a conversation with the chief of staff of the division, *SS-Stubaf.* Conrad, Baum sought to sum up the situation.

**A *Götz von Berlichingen* grenadier.**

**A well-camouflaged *s.I.G.33* artillery piece.**

*"At this time, the Allies are concentrated on Cherbourg, so we can breathe a bit"* began Conrad.

*"We can take advantage of that to establish a continuous front line and try to reinforce the base of the peninsula'* replied Baum.

*SS-Stubaf.* Le Coq, the intelligence officer, then weighed in: *"Our division is holding a front of about thirty kilometers, as far as the Vire. It is a strange piece of ground: except for the road that runs from Carentan to Périers and a few hills, all of the swampy ground is now under a meter of water. The only things that rise above it are foliage, a few wooded areas and a house every so often. It is ground that is almost impassable by armored vehicles but ideal for infantry. There is not enough artillery, except for a few 88 mm anti-aircraft guns. Our grenadiers can count only on themselves".*

Baum carefully examined the maps, trying to find a solution. The only thing that could be done was to delay the Allied advance as long as possible. Only with the arrival of the two *Panzerdivisionen* that had been promised by Field Marshal Rommel could there be some chance to salvage the situation. In the meantime, the Americans had taken control of the canal's lock gates and the water level began to ebb. Special mine-clearing tanks were deployed to clear the minefields, which opened the way for Allied infantry units.

*"What are the unit deployments?"* Baum asked Conrad.

*"The left flank consists of the two remaining parachute battalions, the two grenadier battalions of the 37th Regiment, an army engineer battalion, the march battalion from the school at Angers, the Kampfgruppe under Oberst Heintz (275.Inf.Div.), and on the right is the I Battalion of the 38th Regiment"* replied Conrad.

In reserve was *III./SS-Pz.Gr.Rgt.38*, expected to arrive at any minute. The battalion arrived on 20 June and was positioned south of Tribehou to act as the divisional reserve.

*"We will regroup at Tribehou, ready to intervene if the defensive front should collapse"* ordered *SS-Staf.* Baum.

*"We have to get back our recon group that left the Balleroi forest area northeast of Saint-Lô, and our* Flak *battalion is still at Saumur protecting the bridges over the Loire, and we also have to get our anti-tank battalion which is still waiting for its equipment"* replied Conrad again.

As of 20 June, command of *LXXXIV.Armee-Korps* was assumed by *General der Infanterie* Dietrich von Choltitz, a valorous combatant. That same day, the *Kriegstagbuch* of *A.O.K.7* carried the following: *"... In front of the sector defended by 17.SS-Panzer-Grenadier-Division, enemy movements with tanks in the entire area around and to the east of Cartentan, as well as an increase in patrol activity and activity by assault troops and violent artillery fire, lead to the supposition that the enemy intends to attack west of the Vire. Nevertheless, today, 20 June, there was no offensive action".*

## Notes

[1] Wilhelm Schlebes, born on February 15, 1913 in Bocholt, SS Number 83 224. He had served previously as commander of *3./SS-Aufkl.Abt.6*.

[2] Christian Reinhardt, born on July 10, 1913 in Klein-Kiesow, SS Number 24 813. He had served previously in *4./Sta."Deutschland"* (1936), in *Der Führer* regiment (1940) and as *adjutant* of *SS-Kav.Rgt.1* (1941).

[3] Fritz v. Boeckmann, born on October 9, 1919 in Königsberg, SS Number 391 875. He had served previously in *3./Deutschland* (1941) and as commander of *3./SS-Pz.Gr.Btl."Narwa"* (1943).

[4] Hans von Seebach, born on June 30, 1912 in Stöckte-Hamburg, SS Number 202 333. He had served previously in *Flak-Abt. "Ost"* (1941) and in *3./Begl.Btl. RFSS* (1942).

[5] Erich Hütt, born on May 19, 1925 in Giessen, SS Number 476 648. After having served in *SS-Pz.Au.E.Rg*t, he was transferred to *SS-Pz.Jg.Abt.17* in June 1944.

[6] Helmuth Wagner, born on May 3, 1919 in Augsburg, SS Number 400 147. He had served previously in *14./SS.Inf.Rgt.11* and in *6.SS-Geb.Div."Nord"*.

[7] Hans Samek, born on December 13, 1919 in Vienna, SS Number 473 812. He was transferred to the *2./37* after having attended the *SS-Junkerschule* in Braunschweig.

[8] Karl-Heinz Nieschlag, born on June 27, 1914 in Hannover, SS Number 257 862. He had served previously in *12./Deutschland* (1940).

[9] Horst Rehtmeyer, born on April 11, 1915 in Berlin, SS Number 277 070. He had served previously in the *LSSAH* (1934), in *10./Inf.Rgt.7* (1941) and as commander of *13./SS-Geb.Jg.Rgt.11*.

[10] Otto Baum, born on November 15, 1911 in Stetten-Hechingen, SS Number 237 056. He had served previously in *5./Sta."Germania"*, as commander of *7./LSSAH*, of *III./SS-Tot.Inf.Rgt.3* and of *SS-Tot.Pz.Gr.Rgt.1*. On December 26, 1941 he was awarded the German Cross in Gold, on May 18, 1942 with the Knight's Cross and on August 12, 1943 with the Oak Leaves.

## Bibliography

M. Afiero, *"17.SS-Panzergrenadier Division Götz von Berlichingen"*, Associazione Culturale Ritterkreuz
M. Afiero, *"The 17th Waffen SS Panzergrenadier Division Götz von Berlichingen"*, Schiffer Publishing
Jean Mabire, *"Les SS au poing-de-fer"*, J. Grancheur Editore
J.C. Perrigault, R. Meister, *"Götz von Berlichingen, Vol. 1 e 2"*, Editions Heimdal
Hans Stöber, *"Die Sturmflut und das Ende: band I"*, Munin Verlag

# Hungarian Armored Forces in WW2

by Eduardo Manuel Gil Martínez
(Translated by José Antonio Muñoz Molero) – 3rd part

**Autumn 1944: view of a Hungarian M40 Turan tank, having crossed an improvised field bridge (*The Tank Museum*).**

**A Hungarian 40 M Nimród, Autumn 1944.**

## Debrecen, the gate towards Budapest

Between October 6th and 29th, the battle for Debrecen took place. There the Germans supported by the Hungarians tried to stop again to the Soviets belonging to the 2nd Ukrainian Front under Malinovsky command and its Romanian allies, that this time were trying to annihilate the Hungary's eastern defenses. A Soviet Cavalry Group managed to penetrate the Hungarian defenses to reach Debrecen. But there they encountered a powerful German force that was concentrating there to participate in a counteroffensive called operation "Zingar Baron" ("*Zigeunerbaron*" in German) that should repel the Soviets from the south of the Carpathians. Among the Hungarian armoured units that participated in the defense of Debrecen, was the 16th Assault Artillery Battalion equipped with ten Turan 75 and two Turan 40. On 10 October, despite their bravery, they were forced to retreat to Soviet tanks. The next day, again the 16th Assault Artillery Battalion together with German infantry troops and tanks belonging to the 23rd Panzer Division made a counterattack, succeeding in stop the Soviets. These battles would continue on the 13th and 14th, getting only slow the Soviet advance. On October 19, the 16th Assault Artillery Battalion was ordered to retire in the direction of Polgár (along the Tisza River) after having lost no less than 600 men and a a lot of of its armored vehicles. After the Magyar retreating, between the 19th and the 20th, it would be three Romanian divisions that will eventually conquered Debrecen after a joint assault.

**Autumn 1944: German *Sturmgeschütze* move forward during a counter-attack in Hungary, bypassing captured Soviet Soldiers (*Ullstein Bilderdienst*).**

**Fine close-up of a Hungarian Toldi I light tank.**

**Hungarian M40 Turan medium tank, followed by a field car, Autumn 1944 (*The Tank Museum*).**

The Battle of Debrecen had concluded with a tactical victory over the Soviets and Romanians who had suffered a high number of human casualties and vehicles. But it had not finished the Soviet pressure on the battered troops of the Axis since the advance of these continued. After the victory in the battle for Debrecen, the Soviet troops and their Romanian allies proceeded to eliminate all the German and Magyars troops that still remained fighting in northern Transylvania. The Soviets were advancing from all directions over the territory of the Reich and its Hungarian ally. At the same time as the events cited above, during the second half of October, the 1st Ukrainian Front and the 4th Ukrainian Front participated in the attack on the Ruthenian region and on Slovakia. Finally on October 29th, the Red Army began its offensive against Budapest with more than 1 million of men divided into two attack Groups that converged in the Hungarian capital in order to isolate it from the German and Hungarian forces that still resisted in the Country. Meanwhile, during the second half of November 1944, some reinforcements of men and vehicles for the 2nd Armoured Division continued to arrive like a dropper; these ones were delivered near Párkány (Sturovo, Slovakia). The 3rd Tank Regiment reached 9 Pz IV H and 2 Toldi; and even the crews of the Turan were prepared for their next conversion to the most powerful Pz IV. The 2nd

Armoured Division maintained several clashes in the attempt to avoid the siege of Budapest in the vicinity of Ipolyság (supported by a regiment of the notorious *SS Sturmbrigade Dirlewanger*). This locality was captured by Russians definitively on December 14, 1944. Then the 2nd Armoured Division continued between 9 and 19 December with new clashes in Lovasbéreny. At the beginning of December, the Division was practically decimated, as it had about 119 armoured vehicles, although working only 17. The vehicles were 26 40M Nímrod, 8 39M Csaba, 35 40M Turan 40, 8 41M Turan 75, 16 38M Toldi, 1 Pz III, 20 Pz IV H, 4 Panther and 1 StuG III.

Hungarian M40 Turan medium tank, passing through a Hungarian village, Autumn 1944 (*The Tank Museum*).

German armoured vehicles in Hungary, late October 1944.

Hungarian soldiers on a defensive position with a 7,5 cm Pak 40 antitank gun in a Budapest suburb, 1944.

At the end of the month, more than 100 of these vehicles had been completely removed from the service (in fact by December 21, only remained ready for combat of German origin in the 2nd Hungarian Armoured Division 2 Panther and 2 Pz IV H).

## The Siege of Budapest

October 29th can be considered the start of the offensive against the Hungarian capital and by November 7th the Soviets reached the suburbs of the Hungarian capital about 20 kilometres from it. On December 9th began the preparation of the siege of Budapest, and finally on December 19 the final Soviet-Romanian assault of the city happened. Several elements of the 1st Armoured

Division and from Hussars Division together with the remains of 6 Assault Artillery Battalion as well as other Hungarian and German troops were besieged in Budapest on November 23, 1944. Among the German troops were the remains of the 13th Panzer Division, the 60th Panzergrenadier Division "*Feldherrnhalle*", 8th SS Cavalry Division "*Florian Geyer*" or the 22nd SS Cavalry Division "*Maria Theresia*". These units were that allowed to resist the initial Soviet onslaught against the Hungarian capital.

**A German Tiger and a Hungarian Nimrod anti-aircraft tank in Budapest, October 1944.**

**Hungarian Arrow Cross militia and a German Tiger II tank in Budapest, October 1944 (*Bundesarchiv*).**

The 1st armoured Division had 7 tanks, 3 anti-tank guns and the 1st Hussars Division had only four armoured vehicles. The 6 Assault Artillery Battalion (1st , 7th , 10 and parts of the 13th , 16th and 25th ) were integrated in the "Group Billnitzer" that had about 30 assault artillery vehicles (StuG III, Zrínyi and Hetzer) and 8 75 mm anti-tank guns. In addition to this group were joined some newly manufactured Zrínyi from the factory Ganz that was still working in the same city. As there were more troops than vehicles, many of the crews of armoured vehicles were used as infantry troops.

Hungarian soldiers armed with *Panzerschreck*, Autumn 1944.　　A German *StuG.IV*.

Two Nimrod 40M open firing enemy direction, 1944.

A Hungarian tankman in Budapest, 1944.

The 10th Assault Artillery Battalion and a battery of the 1st Assault Artillery Battalion held a counter attack on a Soviet bridgehead in Baracska on December 8, 1944, which managed to repel the Soviets by making them retreat almost to the Danube, north of Ercsi. Just three days later, on December 11th, the battery of the 1st Assault Artillery Battalion and vehicles belonging to 10th Assault Artillery Battalion were combating in the streets of the city of Erd to the south-west of Budapest. Within the armoured forces that fought in Budapest, we must remember those of the gendarmerie. These counted 10 of the obsolete Ansaldo (years ago removed from the first line of combat), 10 Toldi and 10 Csaba. They also carried out attacks on the Soviet troops in Vecsés on November 1, 1944 with disastrous results. During the months of November and December troops belonging to the Assault Artillery Battalions lacking their vehicles, they fought on foot to the enemy in the area of Vecsés-Maglad-Ecser, in the vicinity of Pest, together with 1st Hungarian Armoured Division. The attacks and counterattacks were repeated in the whole line of the front, recovering and losing a few hundred meters in each one of them.

**The obsolete Ansaldo tanks in Budapest, Autumn 1944.**

**Hungarian infantry with German *Panzerfaust*, 1944.**

**A Hungarian PzKpfw.IV in combat, January 1945.**

The attack from the east towards Pest increased the pressure on the defenders every day. Thus on December 28, the bulk of the "Group Billnitzer" was available in the area of Kispest, in the Magyar capital. On the same day, after unsuccessful attempts to stop the enemy offensive, the remains of the 1st and 13th Hungarian Assault Artillery Battalions that were arranged between Pécel and Ferihegy had to retreated by being unable to close the gap that had left the 8th SS Cavalry Division *"Florian Geyer"* after his retreat. On the other hand, armoured from the 16th and 24th Hungarian Assault Artillery Battalions, managed to maintain their positions in Rákoskeresztur and Újmajor. The same day, the areas to the east and southeast of Pest, Maglód and Gyál were already in Soviet hands. Thus on December 31st near Rakóskeresztúr, the armoured vehicles belonging to 24th Assault Artillery Battalion commanded by Barnabas Bakó managed to reject a Soviet attack causing numerous casualties.

On December 14th, in the face of the imminent arrival of the Soviet-Romanian tide at the center of Pest, the "Group Billnitzer" was called to seal the Grand Boulevard (it was the fifth defensive line in Pest's), with the armoured vehicles and crews that still were ready to fight. But the new Soviet attack provoked the retreat to Buda after crossing the Danube. The "Group Billnitzer" was highlighted immediately in the western part of Buda, to defend the suburbs of this zone just in front of the Soviet advance. For his part the 1ˢᵗ Armoured Division had lost its few armored during the fighting, acting its men as infants during the rest of the siege.

A German PzKpfw.IV on the Hungarian front, crossing an improvised field bridge, January 1945.

A *Waffen SS* soldier in Budapest, with a *Panzerfaust*.

A PzKpfw.IV with infantry aboard, January 1945.

On January 25th, armoured vehicles belonging to "Group Billnitzer" supported by German infantry intervened in the zone of the railways in Lágymános trying to take without success a factory of uniforms where many defenders had been besieged on their upper floor.

The desperate situation, in the frustration of the operations *Konrad* I, II and III of rescue motivated that the commander of the city, the *SS-Obergruppenführer* Karl von Pfeffer-Wildenbruch, ordered on February 11 that the survivors of the siege will try to break it. So the remains of the "Group Billnitzer" and without their armor, were part of the attempt to escape from the Castle Hill.

Only a few of the besieged were able to reach the German lines after many difficulties.

A PzKpfw.IV column on the Hungarian front, 1945.

A Hungarian Toldi I light tank in the mood, 1945.

One of the few pictures where we can see the *Hetzer* using Magyar emblems (*Courtesy of Károly Németh*).

A German assault gun on the Hungarian front, January 1945.

## 1945. The swan song of the Hungarian armoured forces

At the beginning of January 1945 a small combat group from the 2nd Armoured Division was subordinated the Szent László Division which took part in the battle for Garam River. The 3rd Tank Regiment had 3 38M Toldi and 2 Pz IV H. The 52nd self-propelled anti-aircraft artillery Battalion had 7 40M Nímrod. It's possible that all the Zrínyi still operational of the various Assault Artillery Battalions were transferred to battalions 20 and 24th Assault Artillery Battalions during January 1945. On January 1, Tarczay was promoted to captain after which he was entrusted with the mission of moving with 40 of his men to Galánta (Galanta, Slovakia) where they collected on January 8, 1945 some new armoured vehicles for the 2nd Armoured Division. They were 27 Pz IV H (and according to some sources would have to add 2 Panther) that would serve to give some combative value to the 2nd Armoured Division. In order to liberate Budapest, the operation *"Konrad"* was developed in January 1945, which had three phases, called *Konrad I*, *Konrad II* and *Konrad III*. The Hungarian participation in these operations was quite marginal, the most important being the performance of the 2nd Armoured Division with 15 Pz IV H and some other vehicles, which took part in Operation *Konrad* I between 7 and 12 January 1945 in Székesfehérvár. On January 16th, the 2nd Armoured Division already reinforced with the 27 Pz IV H, in addition to 5 Nímrod, 1 Panther and some other vehicles was prepared for the immediate fighting that awaited them. On January 24th, the 2nd Armoured Division, together with the 4th German Cavalry Brigade, supported the attack of the 1st Hussars Division in the Vértes Mountains. The Hungarians attacked in Csákvár with 11 Pz IV H and 4 Nimrod.

**German Panzer and assault gun in the village of Szomor in Hungary, January 1945.**

**German troops in Székefehérvár, January 1945.**

The continuous clashes were destroying the few armored vehicles that remained ready for combat in the 2nd Armoured Division. At the end of February they tried to form a defensive line near of Székefehérvár and Zámoly (near of Lakes Balaton and Velence). 3/II Tank Battalion with 15 Pz IV H fought in Zámoly against the superior Soviet troops willing to take Hungary definitively. The 2nd Armoured Division with 16 Pz IV H, 4 batteries and 4 Motorized Battalions was subordinated to the IV SS Armoured Corp.

**A Sherman Soviet in Hungary, March 1945.**

**A PzKpf.IV Ausf G on the move, March 1945.**

**A Hungarian Zrínyi in combat, 1945.**

On March 17, 1945 Tarczay again took part in the combats commanding 4 Pz IV H near the village of Söréd where they would face 20 Sherman Soviet. In the retreat, the Hungarian ace was killed by the wounds received. Despite the critical situation, the Hungarian armoured units still kept a good number of vehicles in service. So part of the 25th Assault Artillery Battalion was still fighting during March. The 25th Assault Artillery Battalion had on March 15, 1945 38 assault tanks (especially Hetzer), although only six were operative.

The last great attempt to stop the Soviet advance in Hungary was called Operation *"Spring Awakening"* (*Unternehmen Frühlingserwachen*) and is known as Lake Balaton offensive too. In this action, Hungarian armoured didn't take part. Although in the vicinity of the lake, one of the last Hungarian armoured units was still fighting: the 20th Assault Artillery Battalion, which had towards the end of February of 1945, 8 Hetzer working.

During March, the Hetzers belonging to the 20th Assault Artillery Battalion held numerous clashes against the Soviets.

On 21 March, the 20th Assault Artillery Battalion was removed from the front line with only thirteen Hetzers still ready for combat. In the last two months of the war the Hungarian armoured vehicles that were still fighting, did it in small number scattered by various parts of the front. On March 21st the last operating Zrínyi belonging to the 24th Assault Artillery Battalion surrendered in Bratislava, Slovakia, as well as a handful of Turan I survivors. The Soviet avalanche and the lack of fuel caused that during the escape to the north of the country some of the few Hungarian armoured vehicles were abandoned still in conditions to fight, while they tried to reach the German Reich fleeing from the Soviets.

**General Model inspect a Turan Tank, 1944.**

## Conclusions

Hungary had a complicated role during the Second World War, as paradoxically its main rival (Romania) turned out to be another ally of the Axis. So the Royal Hungarian Army was used in the USSR and not against its neighbours, despite the important distrust they had against Romanians. During the global conflict, Hungary not only managed to organize its mobile forces, but developed its own military industry that was able to supply national armaments and equipment to its troops. The Hungarian military industry was able to produce all kinds of weapons, vehicles and armoured vehicles. However, the armoured vehicles carried out by Hungary were outdated from the very moment they were sent to the troops, being unable to fight against the powerful Soviet enemy during all phases of the World War. Hungary could only have first-level armoured vehicles, thanks to which Germany provided them, among which were some specimens of the mighty Tiger and Panther, although in such small quantities that they couldn't be decisive. The arriving of the war to Hungary prevented the development of the latest designs of Hungarian armoured, which very possibly having seen the active service would have been found in conditions quite more couples with their Soviet opponents. The Hungarian armoured forces had to oppose one of the most formidable rivals of their time, the Red Army. Technical failures and tactics were evident from the beginning of the operations. However the troops gave the best of themselves against all odds. They came into combat knowing that even the heaviest anti-tank weapon they had had very little chance of damaging the Soviet T-34, which was not very promising. In spite of this, these men faced their enemies until the end, already in Hungarian lands. After the war only a few members of the Hungarian Army were accepted into the new army, the so-called Democratic Army, most of them were demobilized and retired from Army. The less fortunate were arrested for years, some of them being even executed by the communist regime. I hope that this text will serve to better know this story and reflect the bravery with which the Hungarian army behaved in spite of the difficult circumstances that they had to face.

### Bibliography

Csaba Becze, *"Magyar Steel"*, Stratus. 2006.
Denes Bernád, Charles K. Kliment, *"Magyar warriors. The history of the Royal Hungarian Armed Forces 1919-1945. Volume I and II"*, Helion & Company. 2015, 2017.
Attila Bonhardt, *"Zrínyi II assault howitzer"*, PeKo Publishing. 2015.
Eduardo Manuel Gil Martínez, *"Fuerzas acorazadas húngaras 1939-45"*, Almena. 2017.
Peter Mujzer, *"Huns on wheels"*, Mujzer&Partner Ltd.
Steven J. Zaloga, *"Tanks of Hitler´s eastern allies. 1941-45"*, Osprey Publishing. 2013.

# SS-Hauptsturmfuhrer Hans-Jörg Hartmann
# III Batl. 'Nordland' regiment 5th SS division "Wiking
### By Ken Niewiarowicz – 2nd part

This is a photo-essay based on a stack of Photo albums and documents from the estate of *SS-Hstuf.* Hans-Jörg Hartmann, born in Berlin-Licterfeld on October 21, 1913. The associated text is drawn from the captions of the photos as well as information in the documents that are associated with this grouping.

The following photographs are in chronological order as they appear in the 2 wartime photo albums. These two photo albums were compiled from photographs Hartmann took between June and November 1941 while commanding 12th company in the campaign in the Ukraine. Hartmann recorded the scenes in the weeks following the opening of operation *Barbarossa* in much the same way as many Germans did. The curious nature of the land and the people; the open expanses of the Ukrainian plains; broken vehicles and equipment remaining as the residue of a retreating Red Army.

Hartmann with his *"Befehlwagen"* (On a misty morning, presumably at the beginning of *"operation Barbarossa"*). The cigar is ever present.

Hartmann's driver and batman at the wheel of the KDF type 82.

The cigar is ever present.

June 29; seven days after the beginning of "*Barbarossa*"; Crossing the border into Soviet Ukraine. Each of the vehicles bears the circular swastika emblem of the 5th SS panzer division "*Wiking*" as well as the large stenciled "K" letters identifying them as belonging to "*panzergruppe Kleist*"; named for the commander, Field Marshall Ewald Von Kleist.

**12th company vehicles at the head of the column.**

Along the rollbahn heading south to L'vov. Passing scenes of destruction caused by the leading elements some days before.

Zhovka ancient city gate; 30kms north of L'vov. Note the Ukrainian language banners prepared and hung above the gate; welcoming the German "*Liberators*" with the greeting "*Heil Hitler*".

The lead vehicles first meeting with a Soviet 52 ton tank.

This photo is captioned as "*The Murder building*". A Church in L'vov; reportedly the location of atrocities committed by the G.P.U. (The Soviet state political directorate).

A soviet *KV-2* 52 ton tank with a 15cm cannon. Note the Black & White Swastika identification banner displayed on the hood of the *Volkswagen*; at this point in the campaign the *Luftwaffe* enjoyed almost total air supremacy.

The advance continues north of Tarnopol. It was at Tarnopol that Units of "*Nordland*" caught up with the front-line and first encountered the red army. The scene is one which was ubiquitous in the Ukraine during the summer of 1941; German columns following the non-improved roads which stretched to the far-flung horizon.

Artillery preparations set against a barren landscape.

A striking photograph offering a clear close-up of the blurred edge SS camouflage smocks and various personal equipment.

The first prisoners taken after closing a major pocket of resistance north of Tarnopol.

DKW 350 motorcycle with dispatch rider. Note the large "K" painted onto the fuel tank.

in World War Two 1939-1945

Destroyed enemy armor at Tarnopol. The giant KV2 tanks were a curiosity to the Germans whose own tanks were of roughly half the weight of the soviet monsters.

Knocked out Soviet T-34/76; smaller in numbers during the first year of the war yet highly efficient due to their mobility and striking power.

Zhitomir was heavily contested by the Red Army. The buildings show the effects.

Lead vehicles passing a T34/76 while moving through Zhitomir.

Another T34/76 knocked out 50 meters further down the road. According to the caption: *"The work of German Stukas"*.

An MG nest in a corn field.

*(To be continued)*

WW2 AXIS
FORCES